Longing For The Spirit

Messages of Faith and Hope from beyond the Bottle

Longing for The Spirit

*Messages of Faith and Hope
from beyond the Bottle*

by

Paul Silva

(C) 2017 by Paul Silva

Published by **MERAKI HOUSE PUBLISHING INC.**

All rights reserved. This book or any portion thereof may not be reproduced or used in any manner whatsoever without the express written permission of the publisher except for the use of brief quotations in a book review.

For any information regarding permission contact
Paul Silva via

psilva99@rogers.com

Printed in the United States of America
First publication, 2017.

Paperback ISBN 978-1-988364-23-0
eBook ISBN 978-1-988364-24-7

Book cover design by
www.designisreborn.com

Dedication

To my darling wife **Hina** — my kindred spirit, my greatest ally and the angel who continues to tug at my soul with her light touch.

To my boys **Yusef** and **Imran** for teaching me the right way to live life — with laughter and wide-eyed joy.

To my parents **Rosalia** and **Joe** for their gentle and kind hearts extended in love unbound.

"We are so small between the stars, so large against the sky"
~ **Leonard Cohen**

Contents

Foreword ix
Preface xv
Introduction xix
Lining Up the Shots 28
    The Tunnels 29
    Uncle Miguel 37
    Black Creek, White Light 43
    My Life as a Comic Book Dog 49
    Mr. Fracassi 55
    The Bus Rye-d 61
    Marked Man 67
    The Dragon's Keeper 75
    Hidden 83
    Folding, Unfolding 89
    The Score 93
    Cerveza, Por Favor 103
Anger - Forgiveness 112
    Semifreddo and the Art of Digging Two Graves 113
    Disservice with a Smile 120
    Fair's Fare 125
    Ones and Zeroes 131
Selfishness - Generosity 138
    The Window Played to the Scene of Me 139
    Keys to the Vault 145
    Can't Talk Now I'm Putting my Halo in with the Delicates 151
Deception - Honesty 156
    Myth Busting with a Rocket Launcher 157
    I'm Fine (I Want to Die) 162

    Changing History 169
    A Scattering of Dubious Intentions 179
Arrogance - Humility 185
    I Don't Have Contempt Prior to Investigation,
    I Just Don't Like what I Don't Like 185
    More than a Bushel Full of Brains 191
    Takeout for One 199
    Street Sweeper 205
Insecurity - Acceptance 210
    Dodging and Burning 211
    The Fire Inside 219
    What the General Said 223
    Man Up, Buttercup 229
    Clamming Up 235
Isolation – Service 242
    The Bubble 243
    I Don't Need You 251
    Lone Wolf 257
    Spider in a Box 263
Fearfulness - Faith 270
    Painting Spaces 271
    Leap 279
    The Pity Patter of Self Defeat 283
    The Place Where I Met Myself 289
Resistance - Surrender 293
    The Sentencing and the Veil 295
    Handing Over the Keys 305
    Compliant to Verbal Commands 311
    Closing Windows 317
Loneliness - Community 324
    Eskimo Angels 325
    Slow Ripening Fruit 331
    Redwoods 339
Worthlessness - Hope 343
    What is Your Favourite Colour? 345
    I'm Not What I Am Not 351
    Hideous Me, Glorious Me 357
    Compare and Despair 363
    Peeking Through Joy's Window 373
ACKNOWLEDGMENTS 377

Foreword

I'm not a nut, but sometimes a *literal* nut can be a good teacher. Cashews are simply the most divine nuts that exist on the planet Earth. Although not truly a "nut" in the botanical sense, the cashew is a seed that holds this nut moniker for the sake of culinary simplicity since it both looks like a nut and tastes like one, too.

Personally, I could devour a whole container of these little delicacies in one sitting. I'm ashamed to admit that on occasion I've actually done this. What makes my piggish behavior even more repulsive is the intense labour that goes into harvesting and processing this heavenly fare I so easily and thoughtlessly devour.

I only recently learned that, unlike most other seeds that grow on the inside of the fruit, cashew nuts grow on the outside. The "nut" hangs as a weird little appendage from the bottom of an even stranger looking "fruit" called a cashew apple. They both come from the cashew tree, which grows in warm, tropical places like Brazil, Nigeria and India. The cashew apple looks like an oblong yellow squash, and its seed grows from the base as a brownish-grey mass which seems more like a bizarre fungus or diseased malignancy than something you eat. It's altogether unappetizing in appearance. In fact, in its natural state, it's not appealing at all—the shell of the cashew seed contains compounds that cause a contact dermatitis similar to poison ivy. It makes me wonder how the first humans ever figured out a person could eat it at all.

Today, most of the processing is still done by hand (hopefully with gloves for the sake of the workers). After the seed is removed from the cashew apple, it must first be sundried for weeks. Then, each nut needs dehusking, first by steaming to soften the shell, then by removing the husks one by one. For this stage, processors do use a machine, but the poor workers still have to place each toxic seed in the contraption by hand.

The raw nuts are then cleaned and roasted, and peeled again, because each seed is encapsulated in a second toxic membrane. Finally, the finished seeds are sorted for grade, then salted and packaged.

Whew.

Aside from making me feel really guilty every time I eat cashew nuts, learning about this process prompted an idea, or more aptly, a comparison: every alcoholic or addict must venture through an intensive and sometimes strenuous process to find true recovery. In essence, those of us in recovery from addiction are like cashew nuts.

Much like these fruits hanging from an exotic tropical tree, our lives don't seem to fit within the spectrum of the more botanically correct examples we see around us. And when we seek to interact with the world in the only ways we know how, we seem to only poison others with an itchy deterrent.

At some point, we sought a solution to neutralize our disagreeable state. We thought that dousing our lives with a chemical additive might not only cause us to be more presentable, but also might alleviate the irritating character defects we wished to eschew. At first, it seemed to work. After all, we're not idiots. Drug addicts and alcoholics use substances simply because they are an effective, quick "cure" (or at least a temporary solution). *Better Living Through Chemistry* seemed like a good idea.

However, we soon realized that the cure was worse than the disease. Whatever our concoction of choice was (opiates for me), the additives only exacerbated the annoying itch we caused others and ourselves. Just as there seems to be no easy chemical bath in which to dip a cashew nut to make it more palatable, soon we too discovered that the process would have to be labour-intensive to accomplish the ends we knew we could achieve. Like each cashew requires the painstaking phases of drying out, dehusking, washing, roasting and dehusking again, so must each person in recovery come to grips with the unmanageability of a chemical solution and learn to embrace a more rigorous process. For some, like Paul Silva and me, the technique we use is 12-Step recovery. For others, different modalities seem to work. Regardless of the approach a person chooses, work is involved to bear the fruit we know we are capable of producing.

I "met" the author on social media about two years ago. Since then, I believe I can safely say that he has become a friend and an honoured writing comrade-in-arms. Since I have sworn to myself to avoid mixing any more metaphors than a writer possibly can (or should) in the foreword of a book, I'll safely leave to you any and all conclusions a reader may draw from the previous comparison between people who struggle with addiction and a tropical nut.

The point I wish to convey is that Paul Silva is the real deal. The work he has accomplished in this book is as significant as it is groundbreaking within addiction-recovery literature.

With witty prose he unearths both the core struggles every alcoholic or addict realizes and the central truths paving the way through our long-sought attempts to learn how to function as authentic human beings.

The author has managed to share his wisdom through the lens of his own life, giving the book characteristics of a memoir, but it doesn't read like one. Many books in that genre have the potential to become an exercise in self-aggrandizement, or at the very least a tiresome, linear recounting of the author's history. Paul never forces his story to fit yours. His story is his own, but the narrative never fails to strike chords that harmonize perfectly with my own experience as a person living in long-term recovery.

In a nutshell (forgive me—I couldn't resist), *Longing For The Spirit* is a joy to read, not only for the pithy bits of wisdom the author doles out on nearly every page, but also for the clever and often humorous comparisons he manages to weave throughout his story. Of course, he also portrays the very real and often maddening struggle he continues to endure as a wayfarer on this strange and wonderful journey of sobriety. As a fellow writer and recovering alcoholic-addict, I know this is one book I will continue to relish as much as the delectable cashews I often enjoy. Paul's book has also enhanced my understanding of the obstacles a person in recovery from addiction (or a harvester of cashews) has to overcome to obtain the delicious reward.

Daniel D. Maurer

Author of **Sobriety: A Graphic Novel** (Hazelden Publishing, 2014), **Faraway: A Suburban Boy's Story as a Victim of Sex Trafficking** (Two Harbors Press, 2015), **Papa Luther: A Graphic Novel** (Augsburg Fortress, 2016), and of the upcoming book, **Resilience and Spirituality: The Search to Overcome and Thrive in the Face of Hardship or Trauma** (Mount Curve Press, 2017).

Paul Silva

Preface

"The past is a place of reference, not a place of residence."
~ **Willie Jolley**

This is not a drunkalogue.

There are no sloshed soliloquies or glasses splashed with double shots of Hunter S. Thompson or Kerouac-strength tales within these pages. There is no story of me sauntering to the corner shop for a pack of smokes and waking up three days later, out of a black out, stranded on a desert isle wearing a single cowboy boot, a Hello Kitty sundress and a necklace made of human fingers. I never drank with Stompin' Tom Connors at The Only Cafe or single-handedly took on a swarm of bikers on a subway platform, staggering on brandy-induced bravado. I didn't get into showdowns with Shogun warriors in High Park, participate in epic orgies in Rotterdam or streak on the pitch before an FA Cup game in Barcelona. There are no blow-by-blow tales of tragicomic drunken debauchery here.

Those kinds of stories are out there—funny and heart-breaking, with a high wow-factor—but they are not my stories. Those highlight reel stories only serve to remind us that alcoholism can take us down some strange and surreal paths, but they are often the exceptions and not the norm. For every Arthur Bach or Alan Swann, there's a legion of alcoholics who are slowly stripping the skin off of their lives, one sloppy drink at a time, and wallowing in quiet desperation. Most alcoholics die a painful, lonely death—a far cry from the epic swashbuckling episodes that are sometimes offered up in movies or books. Or in our own minds.

We all have our personal stories—tales of family and ancestors etched into us as we grow up, passed down from the generations. I don't remember a lot about my childhood, but I do remember a lot of the stories my parents told my brother and me about themselves or about other family members. Telling stories is an important part of what we do and who we are. We cackle and snort at them at dinner tables, we sing-song them on porches during lazy summer evenings or we whisper them to our kids at bedtime.

My story is mine alone. It is my currency. Whenever I share my story, it's my ticket to self-examination and to see things in a different light. It's a way to observe myself in others and others in myself. My story is a way of making order out of the (seemingly) randomness of events in my life. My story is a stamp of authenticity of my own existence. It's about connection.

The stories in this book are smudged with the hindsight that only comes after sufficient amounts of pain matched with the lessons they provide—lessons that often take a long time to stick. Some of these reflections had their genesis in my *Message in a Bottle* blog. Most are new additions for this book. My story is found here in chunks big and small. The stolen emotional bits, the heavy parts, the unsuspecting flashes of light caught off mirrors—they're all here. There is no chronology to this book, no sequence for the record, but a mosaic of moments.

I have found that people identify more with the hurt and fears underlying our actions and thoughts rather than the behaviours themselves. When we share our vulnerability with others, we move past the external circumstances and find a common denominator. One need not be in recovery or active addiction to relate to feelings of loneliness, self-pity or resentment. It's how we deal with them which puts the window dressing on our stories.

The sections in this book are loosely organized by a tag team of ten character defects/spiritual principles. It is challenging for me to write about a problem without discussing the solution, hence the pairings. The book starts out with a series of childhood moments, which set the emotional foundation for my foray into the darkness of alcoholism and general spiritual unrest. Those events are not the cause for my alcoholism—this needs to be made clear. But they did set the table for my inclination towards the need to drink. They serve as a collage, revealing a greater picture, just as a pointillist painter would render an image using countless pinpoint dots of varying pressure and size. The reader is encouraged to read the book in any manner they choose—whether it be in order, or jumping around from piece to piece.

It's a privilege to share my story. I am grateful to have been able to find peace and contentment, to sit still in the heart of my spirit and to be able to light the path for those who are starting their own journeys. I am equally grateful for the lamplighters in my life who have shone all along, and helped me open my eyes to the beauty of life.

Introduction

It starts with a thirst.

It's an itch that can't be scratched, a spot washed out by the blazing sun, a sound that can be heard but not located. The Thirst starts off small—like an amuse-bouche at an upscale supper club. It wants to be slaked, to feel full in the belly of its mind. The Thirst doesn't start in the throat. It's not about tap water or fire water; it's about the Water of Life. It's a feeling that flits about the edges of our souls. It's the feeling that something is missing, something is blocked out, a piece of the puzzle has gone missing underneath the living room table and has been chewed up by the dog. The Thirst demands more and more. It is never satisfied until it is quenched fully and completely. It continues to burn until it is soothed, until it is matted out and the rough edges smoothed out. The Thirst is a ballbreaker, a ruthless task master and a scorned lover.

The Thirst knows nothing about morals, righteousness or feelings. It just is. It is a thirst for a connection to its source. It's about feeling undivided. The Thirst wants to feel the ground beneath it and know that it has a place to rest and breathe. It is a thirst for completion, for total wholeness and for a sense of wellbeing.

My thirst started as a need in childhood to take things apart and put them back together—to build, to make sense of the objects around me. Scientific curiosity slaked The Thirst with knowledge, with a sense of order, with a precision of putting everything in its place. It grounded me. As I grew older, The Thirst shifted and my need to belong began to unfold. I had a craving to be accepted and seen for who I was.

My book smarts and A+ grades captured the attention from the numerous bullies in my grade school. My quiet nature and weak limbs were classic and standard fodder in the *Hooligan's Roster of Classmates to Terrorize Handbook Volume 1*. It was as easy as finding "pigeon" in an encyclopedia of birds. I quickly learned that being myself equaled pain. I was strong in math, so that equation was an easy one to calculate. I hid myself from others, and in the process started to slowly hide from myself. The Thirst slipped underground with me as well, but it continued to seek.

It was always seeking.

High school was a robust and muscular upgrade of my grade school experiences. Words were harsher, body slams heartier, and the effects of both stung deeper. Insults stuck to me like burrs. My grades dropped dramatically and the idea of suicide was starting to look appealing. It wasn't that I wanted to die, but I just didn't want to live. The Thirst was still nipping at my heart and mind, and it found nourishment in the music I played. The Thirst was placated but not sated. The music spoke to my soul and it lifted me past the taunting and the growing sense of worthlessness. I wrapped myself in half-notes and semiquavers and I put my head down at the rests and bold double bar lines. I disappeared into dissonant chords, and there was no pain even when I was winded from tedious études and relentless rehearsals. Yet, the Thirst was not pleased in playing second fiddle. It wanted more.

I picked up my first drink at the age of 15. It didn't twist me around its finger on the first go. It would take me years before the alcohol dug its talons into me. I knew early on that I would have a relationship with alcohol, but I didn't realize to what extent. I had found an ally, an inanimate and innocuous liquid which would eventually coat the burning of my restless spirit. The Thirst started to shift as I fumbled into my 20s and 30s. It tapped into the rage, the fears, the self-loathing, the self-pity and the utter contempt I carried around with me. The Thirst played to the dark side of me.

My drinking escalated at the slow and steady rate of a fixed-income investment fund—no real spikes, but the return was good. The Thirst was growing in proportion to my internal unrest. I was increasingly restless, unable to contain myself in my own skin, unable to shed the scales. I found ways to blame everyone for my problems. I swam in denial. I sat in my own waste of negativity and hopelessness. I prayed daily that cancer would strike me down, or a bus. I learned to see myself as something I scraped off the bottom of my shoe. I learned to live by only existing. I isolated myself. I moved further and further away from the Light of the Creator, and into the darkness of countless Guinness Stouts.

Drinking wasn't a means to an end; it was the end. Everything else *was* merely a vehicle to bring me to the barstool. I didn't drink to drink, I drank to get drunk, to taste oblivion and to flirt with omnipotence. I wanted to blot out the existence of me. I wanted to wash the me off of myself. I wanted to disappear and spread out into nothing. The Thirst clutched onto my need for self-destruction, and kindly obliged in orchestrating more self-flagellation. My tolerance for alcohol grew, as did my ability to endure and to administer pain. I relived every harsh word people slashed me with, every scratch across my face, every shot to the soul that I could churn up from my past. I played those tapes over and over again in my mind, feeling the searing jolts from them until I could no longer breathe, hold a thought or even rest my head at night. Alcohol helped to both amplify and deaden those old harms. I didn't see the wounds I inflicted on myself and others during my drinking days. I was too wrapped up in the sweaty cling film of my self-induced grime.

People often say that they have a drinking problem. I didn't. I could drink like a champ; I had the bottles and bruises as evidence. Drinking wasn't my problem—it was my solution. If I didn't have alcohol, I would have thrown myself under a subway train a long time ago. The need to get out of my mind was eased by a few drinks. Alcohol saved my life in many ways.

The solution worked because it worked until it no longer worked. It worked until the solution started to become a greater problem—a second tumour growing on the first one. Loss of lucid judgment, of integrity, of any character I had left in me—these were further casualties of my drinking ways. My soul was as dulled as my mind and my speech.

My world started to collapse within itself in the last few years of my drinking. The façades fell, the self-loathing and self-pity seeped from my eyes and the poison was soaked up in my cells for too long to hold up any semblance of a properly functioning human being. I was fractured and broken. I had isolated myself from most people, and my family and co-workers were confounded by my behaviour. I sat in many soft office chairs paying my therapist to listen to me talk about myself, littering my words with lies. I danced around the real problem—my thinking, my perceptions and my lack of connection to my authentic self and the Creator. These were never explored because they sat in my blind spot, camouflaged by denial.

The Thirst, even as the bricks of my life fell into dusty piles around my feet, was not satisfied. It pushed me further into darkness to drink deeper and to give every part of myself away. It would consume me, even if it meant that it would die along with me, its host. The Thirst was relentless in slaking itself.

Dr. Carl Jung, in a well-known letter to Bill Wilson, co-founder of Alcoholics Anonymous, described the craving for alcohol as "the equivalent on a low level of the spiritual thirst of our being for wholeness, expressed in medieval language: the union with God." He further writes about walking a path that leads to further enlightenment, whether through an act of grace or perhaps a higher education of the mind beyond the confines of mere rationalism. Jung ends his letter with, "you see, alcohol in latin is *'spiritus'* and you use the same word for the highest religious experience as well as for the most depraving poison. The helpful formula therefore is: *spiritus contra spiritum.*"

Paul Silva

The thirst, *my thirst,* was never about alcohol. Alcohol was a chaotic and greedy substitute—a charlatan. My real thirst was the desire for a connection with the Universal Mind, with Source, with God. I knew this at a deep level without understanding it. Many times, when I was suffering through a hangover, I would absent-mindedly seek out religious books. I didn't know it at the time, but I was seeking beyond the bottle. I was looking for Grace, but didn't understand how to grasp it or how to allow it to wash over me. I fumbled through paragraphs, looking for something between the lines in the text, unconsciously trying to find salvation from my lower self (my ego self, my closed-minded self, my contemptuous self).

What started as a desperate way to put the bottle down has transformed into a journey of delving within—of searching in the spaces between the lines. This journey has been about pulling apart the strands of discontent and discord and weaving a new and lush place to hold myself. It's been about making the changes necessary to affect a new way of looking at, and living, life. It's been about quenching the thirst with deep and never-ending connections with the Creator and other people. Having made these connections, the need to satisfy the *Thirst* with alcohol, other substances or behaviours dissipated. That is where the real metamorphosis happened and continues to march on, with plenty of dips and detours to keep it interesting. The more I deepen and maintain these connections, the more contentment I hold. I feel more whole and complete.

Drinking was merely a symptom of my soul sickness. My longing for the spirit was really a longing for *the* Spirit. It started with an unquenchable thirst.

And now my cup runneth over.

Lining Up The Shots

The Tunnels

The police cornered off the area. My mother and our neighbour ushered a few young children past me and the mob of people watching the cops. I don't recall her calling out to me, but I was entranced by the people going in and out of the townhouse at the corner, just before the tunnels. Officers with stern looks and hats pulled down tight marched to and from the front door. I didn't see blood on the pavement, but I knew there must have been. From what I heard later, blood had been spilled. I also found out that some of the other children had to be washed of it, their clothes stained red. Not their own, but the blood of another.

***

The tunnels were like dividers in our townhouse complex. Each successive building was taller than the other, looking like an elongated but short staircase from the distance, with a tunnel separating each new step. This was 1960s architecture at its most indifferent. The buildings were stale afterthoughts of bricks and metal, the antitheses of the manicured and well-loved homes that stood on the other side of Jane Street. The tunnels, ashen grey caverns punctured through the buildings, were used as shortcuts and walkways to get to and from the backside of the simple complex. There were three tunnels, and all smelled strongly of urine and rotting food.

The tunnels were measurements of bravery and necessity for me. The closest one to my area of the townhouses was christened the First Tunnel. The First Tunnel had the graffiti of the private parts of a man and woman on one side, which we kids giggled at, and it also had the most filth near the open chamber, where the garbage chutes were. Every kid in the complex had heard at least one story of one child who fell down the chute and died by fire or by some great machine which chopped refuse (and small humans) into smaller pieces. The First Tunnel was comfortable and safe. It was a great place to play wall ball, jacks or hockey card games. It also acted as an echo chamber for when we practiced our screeching or sang goofy songs.

The Second Tunnel was a little bit cleaner. It didn't have the character of the other tunnels and we only visited it if we needed to pee really badly or if we were ambitious in our hide-and-seek sessions. This tunnel is where I once committed the crime of snipping exposed telephone wires with nail clippers. I saw an older kid do it and thought it looked like fun. The next day, I hovered behind the telephone repair man as he rewired the box unit. I pretended not to listen as he described in detail to no one in particular what he would do to the person who broke the unwritten sacred code of Thou Shalt Not Sever Comm Units. It was the closest I had danced with the devil, by that point. I had nightmares for weeks, all of which featured this man torturing me and taunting me to call for help knowing I couldn't because the lines were cut.

The Last Tunnel was the end of the line and was rarely visited by the other kids. It connected to another building to which we had no access. It had the most foot traffic and no graffiti. We had the least amount of fun in that tunnel because we couldn't scream in there without a grown-up telling us to keep it down because their baby was sleeping or they were trying to watch *Welcome Back Kotter*. I would visit the Last Tunnel to sit, read and get away from the noise of parents yelling and kids screeching. Sometimes I would just walk back and forth, dragging my hand along the wall to feel the bumps and cavities to feel myself grounded to something and to catch the wind in my pores as it flowed over my face. I would stare at the sky and imagine myself as a balloon, wondering where the wind would take me.

* * *

A car stopped in front of the townhouse by the corner, the one beside the First Tunnel, the townhouse where I passed by hundreds of times, watching the people who lived there watering their plants or just sitting outside having a beer. A woman charged out of the passenger side of the car, her blond hair rustling around her red eyes.

"Oh God! Oh God! Where's my baby? Show me my baby!"

I watched as two police officers grabbed her arms just as she started to fold into herself, knees buckling. There was silence and she cried out again. I left. I wanted my mother. I wanted to see her as badly as this woman wanted to see her child. But I did not cry out. I just left.

* * *

The complex was located next to an area that was infamous for having a lot of trouble. Jane and Finch was a bustling bubble in Toronto, jammed with families of all nationalities and low-income earners. It was also an area crammed with thugs and hotspots for crime and drug use. Refugees and immigrants rubbed shoulders with dealers and gangbangers. Rusted bikes and broken toys littered sun-burnt lawns where teens smoked up or fought one another over perceived slights and dollar bills. I had often walked through the area on my own, with a hockey stick over my shoulder and my head down, waiting until I got to the community centre to join a game of pick up. I avoided the spots of potential danger and dodgy characters, choosing to stay close to the comfort of grass and ground, rather than explore the harsh and jagged unknown.

The large fence which separated us Tunnel Dwellers from the scary Other Side Kids was often the scene of battles, which were as thrilling as they were dangerous. When we had snowball fights with the kids from the other side, we made sure the snowballs had quarter-sized rocks in them. There was a tribal sense amongst both sides, and the intent was to ward off, and even harm, the other warring group. Many went down in these epic battles. Usually, they were called off when there were too many injured on one side, or when frantic mothers called everyone for dinner, waving wooden spoons in the air like magic wands.

One particular afternoon, there was a mysterious supply of roofing shingles scattered on both sides of the fence. This simple offering from parts unknown was the catalyst for a precarious match of throwing ninja stars. There was no snow to cushion blows. Every Tunnel Dweller was on their own to keep the pride of our side protected and unscarred. Shingles flew, slicing the air at every possible angle. Ducking and leaping were requisites to avoid getting stitched up at Humber River Hospital. I had one person in my crosshairs that afternoon: a kid in a tree who was their ace sniper. I loaded up one of my ninja stars and threw it in an arc that nicked the neck of the tree kid. He clutched at his fresh wound and tumbled out of the tree. This signaled the end of the battle. The other kids scattered when they saw the stakes had been raised and no one was safe from potential blood loss.

I felt initial elation at this harm, and yet, a part of me was frightened. Conflict wasn't something that sat well with me. When one of the neighbourhood boys would chase me down or threaten me, I shook for hours after. I felt my tongue swell and my hands stiffen. I had taken karate lessons, but the only thing my legs were good at was running away.

* * *

My mother and our neighbour were giving some of the young children juice and snacks. I was upset because I rarely got juice and snacks. I was told always to wait for dinner. But this wasn't a regular visit. It wasn't like when the neighbourhood kids would smell my mother making tuna pie and drag themselves over like zombies picking up the scent of brains. I grabbed a juice and watched my mother patting the children's heads, shushing meek cries and whispering to our neighbour in staccato tones.

I overheard something about a drunk man. I didn't understand what drunk meant, but it didn't sound good. I heard about a knife. The townhouse at the corner, where the screaming lady was, was a daycare of sorts. My brother and I never went there, but we knew some of the younger kids went. I didn't know any of them, but then again young children all looked the same to me—lost and bewildered with lots of dirty diapers and cheeks that were too big for their faces. I would find out later that the man stabbed an 18-month-old baby to death and injured another. His wife was at the store when it happened, filling up on formula, crackers and baby powder.

After then, I didn't go down to the First Tunnel as much. The gusts in there felt a little colder, a little sharper. I just stayed near my house and threw rocks on the roof, wondering what was on TV and wishing I could stop seeing that blond woman's face in my mind.

Uncle Miguel

My uncle Miguel was the only uncle I had and knew. My mother's brother was alone in the direct uncle and aunt department. Many families I knew were resplendent with cousins and other extended family. My family had always been a tiny clan, and so while we may have saved money on buying gifts and cards for non-existent birthdays and anniversaries, there was always a lack of family members to get to know or build relationships with. So Uncle Miguel was pretty much it, and I loved him and always looked forward to him coming around.

My folks came to Canada from Uruguay in 1969, and my uncle followed a few years later. He lived in an apartment a few minutes away from our townhouse, so he was always available to drop by, as he often did. He and my mother would sit by the back sliding door, the door partially open with the smell of someone's backyard BBQ or the sound of nearby traffic creeping in. My uncle sat with one lanky leg crossed over the other. He stroked his trimmed beard whenever he listened. They would talk for hours about what was happening back home, what was going on in their lives and what plans they had. I listened to my parents' albums while they spoke. Many times, Queen, Styx, The Doobie Brothers and Earth, Wind & Fire music were the uninvited soundtracks to their discussions. While I wasn't focusing on my mother and Uncle Miguel, I still watched them, capturing the lines and expressions on their faces as they spoke, noticing when my mother would reach over and touch her brother on the arm now and then, the sunlight cutting across my uncle's bell-bottoms.

Uncle Miguel was lithe, firm and wiry. He was a 10th dan Shotokan karate practitioner and teacher. He taught me for a short time, but my interest waned after a while—a common theme for me as I grew up. I was always on the lookout for the new shiny thing, to keep me from staying with myself, as myself would prove to be frightening. My real interest at that time was magic, and my uncle would always surprise me with a new magic set, a book or something that would keep me in the magic realm. I believe that he saw something in the fantastic and unexplained that also captured his imagination, and he enjoyed fostering that sense of wonderment in me. He always seemed to be in a state of that wonderment himself, seeking and finding new paths to shiny newness within.

He was aloof at times, yet warm. I don't recall if I hugged him much or if he sought me out for physical affection. But I remember that I just loved to smell him; he smelled of sandalwood incense or other exotic aromas that hung in the air in his apartment like ornaments, all part of his Zen Buddhist practice. His love of embracing and teaching Eastern philosophies and his spiritual traditions manifested in all parts of his life. He showed me the *I Ching*, which I found fascinating with its hexagrams and Chinese symbols and their different meanings. There was a precision there that spoke to me, even if I couldn't make sense of it at the time. He introduced me to *Tintin* and *Asterix and Obelix*, which I reread into my teens and adulthood. Uncle Miguel married a woman from Argentina, and they were childless. We didn't see Aunt Selma often.

Uncle Miguel once came over, his face gaunt and ashen. He was excited, an emotion I rarely saw in him. He had a calming influence on me and others, so to see him worked up made me anxious. I found that even at a young age, I picked up on people's energy and took it on. I was easily influenced by others. He pointed to a hole in his plaid red shirt pocket. He said he had been shot by an air rifle. He wasn't badly hurt, but taken aback enough to involve the police. He later took me to the spot where he got shot and pointed to where he thought the perpetrators may have lived. It was an apartment complex across the street. All apartment complexes looked the same to me—they all had the same drab bricks, the same chipped and faded grey balconies, the same dulled and yellowed fabric curtains covering suitcase-sized windows. I pressed into the hole in his shirt, his large hand guiding my finger. The hole was near his heart, and the pressure broke the skin a little. I thought, "Here's a man who's been shot and lived to tell the tale! He truly was a super man!" My young mind latched onto that image, although I knew it wasn't entirely true I still loved the idea of his invincibility, as I felt anything but. Uncle Miguel was the personification of how I wanted to live. I wanted to be him in many ways.

As the years passed, Uncle Miguel's visits slowed down, and eventually stopped. Something had shifted in his relationship with him and my parents. I didn't ask, or at least when I did my mother would say that he was busy with his new dojo or something simple and soothing. I could tell that my mother was hurt and that she, too, missed his visits. I still listened to my albums, but I now stared at the lyric sheets in the albums, not at the sliding door. What I did know was that my mother's love for him was deep—a type of love that I never could feel towards others or feel even for myself for a very long time. I didn't understand it, but I could feel it emanate from her.

Uncle Miguel was a brilliant man—well-read, eloquent and full of promise. But he was fractured emotionally and wasn't able to fully be there. He was there and yet he wasn't, which is why I can only remember the half-hearted hugs. His affectionate waywardness never gave me a sense of full love, and yet I sensed that he desired it and craved it as much as I did. He couldn't make that final connection, and retreated in so many ways. He was able to give unconditionally to his students, to strangers and to his numerous acquaintances, but was bereft of that same attention to his own family—his adoring, doting sister and wanting nephews. This gradual estrangement was too much for my mother and a breaking of ties was the result. My mother felt his brilliance never fully blossomed, something that I saw in myself many years later.

My uncle died two weeks before I got married, when I was 23 years old. He had a sudden heart attack. We visited him in a private emergency room—tubes, straps and wires littered the floor and Uncle Miguel's body. It was the first time I'd seen dead eyes in a loved one. His vacant gaze cut through me, yet I couldn't react. I was already on my way to my alcoholic self. My feelings and emotional states were already marred by the uncertainty of myself, and the alcohol was already medicating and soothing me. I remember wanting to cry, but unsure if I could. Selma, who was no longer my aunt after she and Uncle Miguel divorced, wailed in the emergency room with emotion I had never witnessed from her usual self. I assumed a position behind her and watched, as if I were watching my dentist work on me or if I were viewing a TV commercial.

    I never had a chance to talk to him about what it was like for him to be him, but I always sensed that my path was like his. The exception was that instead of getting shot near the heart, my heart got a shot it needed to wake up and see things for what they really were, unencumbered by the haze of alcohol and selfishness. But as a young boy all I saw was the beard I could tug on, the biceps on which I could hang off of like a monkey and the amazement on his face as I showed him one of my polished magic acts.

Black Creek, White Light

I kept the LEGO box under my bed. It was a simple construction of tightly pressed coloured blocks with a removable lid. It sat empty and unused until I was inspired to find two unknowing combatants in the field behind our townhouse. I'd put a pair of anything living into that Cube of Doom that could fit into my 8-year-old hands, close the lid and watch through a tiny hole I made to see how they interacted with each other. Grasshoppers, garter snakes, crickets, caterpillars, spiders, centipedes, cockroaches and even the odd moth or butterfly became prisoners in that box. I avoided the bees. I would sit on the grass and peek inside as the wee warriors circled around one another. Most of the time nothing happened. Or, they just tried to find a way to escape. My attempt to create inter-species drama often fell flat. I often shook the box to incite some sort of anger or irritation in the battle partners, but all it did was crush or injure them. On occasion, I witnessed a skirmish or even a rare mortal victory. But mostly there was boredom.

"Oh c'mon, do something!" I would yell and slap at the grass.

Eventually I would release them and find another activity to do, but there was something about trying to cause a disturbance that stayed with me for a long time—a sense that I needed to control things like a James Bond villain, and we all knew villains were more fun to watch than heroes.

* * *

There is an old tale about chaining elephants. If you tie a chain around a baby elephant's back leg, attach the chain to a stake and drive the stake into the ground, the baby elephant is unable to move anywhere. The elephant is chained like this until it starts to grow up and fend for itself. By that time, the elephant has already learned that it cannot go any further than the length of the chain. So, while the elephant is strong enough to pull the stake out of the ground, it doesn't. It has been conditioned to stay as it is. It has been mentally broken down and programmed to remain as it is.

Fences and borders aren't always made of metal, wire or wood. Many of them were in my mind, attached to the length of chain that kept me grounded. The area surrounding our small townhouse was a checkerboard of spaces both wide and tightly portioned. Zigzags of fences and boundaries marked zones into friendly and not-so-friendly duchies. Any time I was pressured by other kids to go off my chain, I would cry because I thought I would get in trouble. I kept to my roster of welcoming areas: the rec centres where I would play sports; the vast grass athletic fields of York University; the strip plaza where I would buy my mother cigarettes; or the place we called "The Rock," where on top of a small hill lay, surprisingly, a stone large enough to be a ship, a castle or whatever a bunch of kids could rally up in their imaginations.

On the other hand, the area where the Rastafarian men sat in the shade and smoked weed all afternoon was a no-go zone. As was the corner unit where the guy exposed himself in too-loose shorts when napping outside, or the ravine area where, according to the older kids, dead bodies were regularly strewn about. I played cricket with the Sri Lankans down the street, softball with the large family from Newfoundland a few houses down and Red Rover with anyone I could wrangle together at the time. I loved when the kids chanted my name to charge over, and I felt a connection to these kids as I broke through their chains of hands, laughing as I fell onto the mud-tipped grass.

We lived behind Black Creek Pioneer Village, a touristy village of authentically restored homes, workshops, public buildings and farms from the 1860s. Our backyard faced the chain-link fence at the back part of the village, the area that paying customers never saw, which was overgrown with bush, wild plants and knotted trees. In wintertime, you could smell smoke coming from olden fireplaces, and at Christmastime, the aroma of orange and clove emanated from the wooden buildings as they adorned them for a festive touch. And while I would easily crawl under the chain-link fence to explore the area, the places I avoided were the ones which were off limits to paying guests and disregarded by staff—the clearings strewn with empty beer bottles, cigarette butts, *MAD* magazines and the occasional torn condom packages. I would rake my fingers over the rough wooden fences constructed near the village, not daring to venture in. I would pet fuzzy caterpillars and rub pussy willows against my cheeks. I would blow white dandelions and caress cattails.

The feeling of being at one with all of this gave me a sense of home; it kept me connected to something. I was alone but not lonely. I wasn't aware of it at the time, but I was already learning that simplicity and living in the present begat serenity and peace of mind. I wasn't weighed down by corrosive thoughts of "What will other people think?" Nor did I compare myself to other kids or try to impress them. I just *was*. And that sensation of *being* felt innate, in line with how I was supposed to feel all along. It was as natural and flowing as the tall grass I would run through whenever I had the chance, dodging darting dragonflies and tiny bouncing frogs. And when the sun rose high, that hot, almost-white light hit me square in the face and I would close my eyes and stare at the red dots in my eyelids. Until I was too tired to even catch my breath, I wished I never had to go home.

My Life as a Comic Book Dog

I devoured *Peanuts* comic books when I was a kid. I was fascinated with Charlie Brown and the ridiculous and rich cast of characters that surround him. Charlie is a walking case study in insecurity and wishful thinking. While he may be the sad sack protagonist in *Peanuts*, the character I loved most was Snoopy and his almost endless imaginative alter egos. The WW I Flying Ace, the World Famous Hockey Player and the World Famous Attorney were some of my favourites. But no one beat Joe Cool. Joe Cool was my pick of the crafty canine litter. I felt a kinship towards the groovy hepdog. I used to flip ahead in the books to see when Joe Cool would be coming up, and read furiously so that I could get to those parts. I would sit in my room for hours reading and rereading *Peanuts*. It was my escape.

When my mother would call us for dinner, it wasn't unusual for me to saunter down the stairs wearing my dad's sunglasses and an over-sized long-sleeved shirt, proclaiming "I'm not Paul, I'm Joe Cool." ("Ok Joe Cool, eat your squash.") I enjoyed absorbing that character and putting my own self to the side, shelving it until Joe Cool was no longer needed, like when it was time to brush my teeth or do homework (Joe Cool never did homework, by the way).

Joe Cool pretended to be a college student, hanging around his dorm (a.k.a. his doghouse) and shooting wide smiles at the ladies when they passed. He often leaned against something to act aloof and distant. He didn't say much, except to declare how cool he was. He was an observer, never a part of the fray and only getting involved when he had no choice. He was detached from the world, too hip to engage in idle chatter, but still hung around. He was often alone. He was a poor man's (dog's?) version of The Fonz.

My fascination with the *Peanuts* gang waned as I grew older. I found other ways to lose myself. But, in a life-imitates-art transformation, I unknowingly took on the persona of Joe Cool: I was always around the action, but not a part of it; I was a spectator of life, rather than diving into it. I sought attention from the wrong people for the wrong reasons. I was aloof and emotionally distant. I acted grandiose and yet felt less than. I watched the action unfold and avoided it, yet secretly desired to be a part of it. I was alone and tried too hard to fit in. I was the poor me's version of me.

The idea of keeping a cool distance and yet wanting to be a part of it all struck something in me. Many times I would hide behind a book at my desk, hoping the teacher wouldn't call on me to answer a question, and yet I felt hurt when they didn't. I felt that I knew the answer better than anyone, yet didn't feel I deserved to be recognized for it. I was like the referee in a game; I was around the action, yet no one noticed me until I made a mistake, at which point I was punished for it. I felt that I wasn't a part of this world, as if I was here on lovely planet Earth just to take notes. Then, when the mothership would come calling, I would have been transported to the planet where I knew instinctively how to live: where I didn't feel estranged playing Frozen Tag or eating Rice Krispies squares with other kids by the newly painted portables. I didn't have that sense of belonging here on Earth.

The grey zone between wanting to be seen and not wanting to be seen was vast and cruel; it created friction within my small, bony frame that I could never seem to smooth out or sand down. I was at arm's length from those around me, but in my mind I was lightyears away. I spent many recesses playing alone, bouncing a worn out tennis ball off the school wall over and over. I would often cast an eye on the group beside me playing marbles, kids squealing and groaning as the cats' eyes clinked against one another on the concrete. The kids all seemed to speak an unspoken, foreign language—a dialect that fostered camaraderie and glee. I ached for that kind of connection—a connection that I would yearn over for a very long time.

It was the first time in my life that I could sense a disconnection between me and others, a self-induced hard page break that kept me apart from the other kids. My story seemed to be unfolding differently, and like Joe Cool and the rest of the *Peanuts* characters, my life was kept constrained in a tiny tier of panels. All I needed to do was to step out of my box and take in the pageantry around me, but there was a concern that I would come to harm. It was easier to eat my cheese sandwich in the corner of the gym, reading up on chess, rather than risk feeling the arm of a classmate around me, pulling me close to give me a hard noogie.

Joe Cool may have been an amusing 2D character in a book, but translated into a 3D Gospel of Being, he was as flat and faded as the paper the comics were printed on. It was a poor way of choosing to be, but it was my way—a way that would dog-ear mark the rest of my childhood and adult life.

Mr. Fracassi

Mr. Fracassi wore a leather coat, snug jeans and aviator sunglasses. He drove a black IROC, the car he sometimes gave me a ride home in after school. Gold chains adorned his neck and rattled with every move he made. He was my Grade 6 teacher, the only male teacher in a Catholic school which taught a large number of Italian-Canadians. There were a handful of non-Italian "others" like me roaming the hallways. Being of Uruguayan descent, with olive skin, dark eyes and even darker hair, it was always assumed I was Paulo, not the Pablo that was stamped on my birth certificate.

Mr. Fracassi, Italian as the *bocconcini* and *salumi* he snacked on while we did our lessons, taught all of our subjects, so we surrounded him all day. During music class, while other teachers taught traditional Catholic hymns, he played The Eagles, Queen and Supertramp. I was thrilled when I was asked to bring in one of my Beatles albums for class. I made sure to carry it very carefully to school the next day. Mr. Fracassi grinned when I handed it over to him, brushing his wide moustache. He threaded the album on the turntable, whistled to himself and then smiled again, patting me on the head, the chains on his wrist jingling near my ears.

I wanted what he had—that ease of being comfortable in his skin, confident but humble. He laughed at everyone's jokes, even when they were terrible. When he listened to someone, he put his hands on his hips and took the person all in with his eyes. I wanted that scent he wore, I wanted that genuine laugh and I wanted to be him, but not be him at all. I wanted to be me, but *more* of me, in the manner that he seemed to be more of himself. It was as if his aura took more space around his toes than so many other people's did around their whole body. Whenever he was upset with the class and assigned us lines to write, I raced against one particular student to be the first one finished. I was often done first and showed him my work, my puny chest puffed out as I marched to his desk. He'd wink at me, tell me to sit down and he'd continue chewing gum and working on a crossword.

It was the first time I could remember seeking someone's approval. I didn't work hard to get my parents' approval—I knew that they loved me unconditionally. They supported me the best that they could. Of course, there were times I did seek their approval. I never raised my voice at them as I grew up, and I did my best to act like the dutiful son and do what they asked of me. It was partly because I wanted to be seen as "good" and not a troublemaker. My younger brother Michael was a spirited and passionate boy, which sometimes led him into situations that didn't serve him well. Or my parents. So I tried to stay in a place of neutrality to stay under the radar.

Mr. Fracassi was the first man that I knew who wasn't blood and towards whom I felt the same affection. He was my unofficial big brother, and I played in his shadow to capture his essence in some ways. It wasn't so much about putting the man on a pedestal as it was recognizing something within him that spoke to me. He was authentic.

He taught us gym, and in one class in particular we played basketball. We ran drills, practiced some basics and then played a scrimmage game. He blew the whistle to signal that we were done.

"Hit the change rooms, guys. Except you four," he said, pointing his finger at three bigger boys and me.

Oh crap, what did I do? Is he mad at us? Is he mad at me?

"Line up, boys," he said, indicating to one of the red lines on the gym floor.

We stood there, the other boys towering over me by at least half a foot. Mr. Fracassi inspected us like he was judging a dog show. He held the basketball under his arm and pushed the aviator glasses up his nose.

He pointed at us, shaking his finger.

"You all have potential. Do you hear that? Potential." He punctuated the last word with his finger, landing on me. He stared right at me and winked.

"You should look into getting on the basketball team. You have something in you, guys. I can see it. I can see that in you, that love, that passion."

I didn't know what to say. I never saw myself as a part of any team. I played ball hockey in the concrete corners of my townhouse complex, or sometimes in other school gyms, but never basketball. I tried not to smile, to let him in on the feeling that I just glowed like I swallowed the moon. I didn't know how to handle someone other than my parents praising me for something I did. But I knew that smiling would make it look like I was surprised. I wanted to act confident, as if I already knew about my flawless execution of the half-court press and about my no-look passing prowess. I stood there and watched the gold chains rattling off his neck as he spoke to us.

He dismissed us, but I felt far from dismissed inside. I was *seen*—a feeling that intoxicated me. It was as if his spirit reached into mine, wrapped its arms around my spirit and held it close. It was an acknowledgment of my very being. It was a fix that I would chase for a very long time in my life. Validation was a buzz.

The Bus Rye-d

The spit landed between my feet.

The Gob Enchantress stood over me, her long, blond-streaked hair partly covering her eyes.

"Looks like sperm, eh?" she said, wiping her mouth.

I stared at the mess on the bus floor and then back at her. She sneered and put her hands in her jacket pockets. She sensed that I wasn't going to retaliate. She was right—I sat there, feeling the weight of my school bag on my lap. It felt like it had thirty bowling balls in it. Embarrassment and humiliation aren't light—they are often carted around long after the humiliating event has happened. And this was just one of many for me.

"I don't know what you-" I started.

"You're a loser! A pussy!"

I didn't say anything after that. I tried not to cry, not to let her see that I *was* a pussy. I didn't want her to see that I didn't understand conflict, that it made me uneasy, or that it tore strips off of me inside. I didn't understand why someone I'd never met before would do that on a bus full of other strangers. Who was she? I didn't want to ask. I wanted the bus to run over me and leave me as a stain on the world, like I felt.

The girl stood there for a few seconds and went back to her friend, who was laughing. They stared back at me and snickered. I sat motionless. I closed my eyes to wash away the scene and to avoid looking at the spit. I got up and walked to the front of the bus. The driver was still letting people on the bus. I hustled past a stroller and a shopping cart.

"Excuse me, but a girl back there spat at me. I don't even know her, but she just spat."

The bus driver looked at me through his rear-view mirror, even though I was standing right behind him.

"What do you want me to do?" he said, readjusting his seat. "I'm not her dad."

"Can't you tell her to get off the bus?" I asked, my voice lowering.

"I can't. She didn't break the law, kid. Just sit away from her."

The bus driver closed the door and eased back into traffic.

I stood there for a few more seconds and then rang the bell. It would take me 15 minutes to walk the rest of the way home, but I couldn't stay on the bus. I got off at the next stop.

"Have a great day," the bus driver said as I landed on the pavement.

Have a great day.

I shuffled into my house and dumped my school bag on the kitchen floor. We now lived in a bungalow in an area that was built in pre-WW II, complete with oil tanks and knob-and-tube wiring. We had a garage and a serviceable backyard. The rooms were small, but the house was just large enough for a family of four.

There was nobody home.

I felt a darkness envelop me that I had never experienced before. There was a despondency within me that free-floated through my spirit and mind. I had been hurt and had felt emotional pain before, but this was different. This had weight to it. It had critical mass and yet no shape or form. I didn't know how to deal with this sudden feeling of despair. I paced back and forth, hoping to shake it off, like when I'd hit my funny bone or stubbed a toe. I couldn't cry. There were no tears at this level of despondency.

I then remembered my parents' liquor cabinet. My folks weren't big drinkers. They would have a beer now and then. The liquor bottles were gifts from other people when they came over. I had never seen my parents take from it, but I knew where it was. I remembered how the grown-ups on TV would, when faced with strife, take a shot of some mysterious brown or beige liquid, often poured from a glass decanter on a mantle. I also recalled the sour face they made after downing the potion. Perhaps it was because the drink worked for them in some voodoo kind of way. I thought that perhaps I could take a bracing shot of something, anything, to help dissolve the darkness.

I scanned the labels: Amaretto, Canadian Club, Sambuca. These didn't mean anything to me. It was like gazing at an alchemist's shelf, wondering which magic mixture would create the perfect solution to turn that poisonous lead in my system to gold. I grabbed the bottle that read "Rye." It seemed the least intimidating and had the shortest name. It had the same clear brown liquid they showed on the TV programs. It would do.

I poured myself a glass and went into my parents' bedroom. I thought that if I were to do a grown-up thing, I might as well do it in a grown-up environment. I closed the door and pulled the drapes. The lights were off. Light seeped in through the window, but it wasn't offensive. I lay there, motionless for a few minutes, as if trying to transpose the weight of my pain onto the bed, to let it spill onto the floor and bleed through the floorboards. I took the drink and smelled it. It had a faint odour of expired milk or my mother's nail polish remover. I didn't let that deter me. I was determined to find my solution. There was no way people could feel what I did and not do anything about it. There had to be a way to numb it all out or to bring some light to it.

I took a sip.

This is often where many alcoholics would recount that this first sip was the magical moment, the game changer that as soon as that liquid hit their bloodstream it seemed to also hit the sweet spot of their soul—that everything seemed to float away and everything in the world just seemed *right*. That was not my experience. As soon as it hit my tongue, I ran to the kitchen sink and spat it out. It was horrid, acrid and medicinal. I went back, grabbed the glass and poured the rest of the rye down the sink. I rinsed my mouth and the glass and I walked back to my own bedroom. I lay down and started to cry, not because I wanted to relieve myself of that darkness but out of shame that I couldn't stomach the alcohol. I felt as if I'd failed once again. Once again, I couldn't seem to figure anything out.

I felt useless in life.

I thought of the girl who spat at me and felt as if I'd deserved it. Those other kids at school wouldn't have taken that. They would have fought. They would have shown that girl that they weren't a pussy. For all my bluster and newly anointed, macho tomfoolery, I was still just a frightened, sensitive boy. I jumped at my own reflection, a reflection I was starting to sneer at and to pity. I wiped the tears and sat up.

I spat in my hand, to feel it again and remind myself that I wasn't worth much. I watched the spit this time; I didn't turn. I needed to see what I was—a wee puddle of nothing. It sickened me. I wiped my hand on my pants and lay down again.

Marked Man

She ripped it out of my hands.

A comic book, tucked into the math textbook we were supposed to be reading, was now crumpled in her crooked fingers. The teacher's face was flush, the lines on her tanned face deep and creased. Her mouth tightened, her lipstick long faded from feeding on her coffee cup. The students in the classroom quieted except for a few snickers that escaped from the back of the class.

"You think you're better than everyone, yes? Don't you, *monsieur?*" she yelled, her thick Parisian accent sharpening the tone.

I didn't answer. I put my head down.

"You go to that school...that, that program. You never say anything to anyone about this. It's like your own little secret, yes?"

She shook the comic book up and down in front of me, as if to fan and cool me down.

Another snicker from the back slowly started to crescendo until a few others joined in and raised it to a small chorus.

The teacher walked back to the front of the class and threw down my X-Men comic on her desk. She wiped her hands on her long sweater, took a deep breath in and continued to teach the class.

I looked at my knees. They were shaking. I knew that the other ones would get me at recess. They always did when they smelled fresh blood.

***

It was the first move that I could remember. When I was a baby, my parents lived in an apartment in the north end of the city, and then moved to the townhouse complex. My school was a safe place. I could be myself. I could be with others or not. I could explore and play and know that what made me stand out was accepted. My friends at St. Augustine Elementary School were as cherished as my neighbourhood friends. My first crush was Nadia, who was in most of my classes. The skies were always clearer, and the sun's heat always warmer, when I was near Nadia. We planned to have a milkshake date at one of the veal sandwich and sub takeout restaurants by the strip plaza, but that never materialized. It may have been a sign, but the restaurant closed just before me and my family moved away.

I was in a gifted program starting in Grade 5. I scored well in a random test and I guess the school board Star Chamber decreed I was fit enough to be pulled out of class once a week to hang out with some other studious misfits at another school. What started as a group of awkward, gangly kids trying to figure out what we were doing there turned into a nerd-laden tribe where everyone looked out for one another.

We were allowed to explore different media and methods of learning. I took apart rudimentary electronic games and put them back together, my tiny fingers careful to put the motherboards back exactly as I found them, not that a nine-volt shock was anything to fear. We solved mind games and puzzles. My need to understand things and categorize them into neat mental and physical boxes was met. I could quantify and qualify things. I was surrounded by others who felt the same. I was challenged. I was free to roam in all ways. I could even go to the washroom without having to raise my hand. I was able to take books out from the adult portion of the library, unlike at the local branch near my house where I was kicked out and told to return to the children's area. I felt grown up. I pictured myself as Truman Capote, complete with an appropriate bow tie and a cigarette lounging in my hand. I laughed a lot, too. We ate our lunches on the floor while doing brain teasers.

I was home.

When we made the move to accommodate my father's work transfer within the city, I continued the gifted program, but in the east end. I was essentially moving to two new schools. While St. Rose of Lima accepted me with open arms, continuing to grow in an unstructured structure with other mini mad scientist types, my reception at my new grade 7 classroom was like being thrown into a vat of battery acid, naked, with raw hamburgers strapped to me and starved pit bulls and piranhas tossed in for good measure. During Lent. Because, during Lent, I couldn't have chocolate, and that was just as bad as the acid bath idea.

***

"Are you that stupid?" he screamed at me in the hallway.

We were alone. His large frame blocked the view to the school board–approved, metal-wired window at the end of the hallway.

"How did you not know this was the right test? You are just in your own little world again, aren't you? You think everything revolves around you, don't you?"

The geography teacher continued to yell at me, his blue tie waving in my face, like a pendulum measuring time. I peered at the open classroom doors on both sides of us. *Everyone is listening to this. I'm dead after school.*

"I didn't know that this was the wrong test. I'm sorry," I replied, talking to the floor.

"That's because you didn't read the goddamned book. You're too busy at that *other* place doing God knows what."

The "other" place. The sanctuary.

"I will do better, sir. I just didn't know. I was busy. I-"

"You get a zero and that's it. No redo!"

He tugged his jacket down and stomped into one of the classrooms. I exhaled. I tried not to cry. Crying was like catnip for bullies. I took another deep breath. I needed to go back to the classroom to get my binder. I braced myself for the muffled, self-righteous laughs. *I'm dead after school.*

I was starting to feel dead all the time. Bit by bit, I was turning to ashes.

* * *

Growing up and around other kids and adults who celebrated differences and showcased one another was the mortar with which my childhood had been slowly built, like a dam or retaining wall.

"Isn't Vincenzo a great runner?" the coach announced as we applauded in the gym.

"Doesn't Alva have a lovely singing voice?" the music teacher decreed as we finished our school play rehearsal.

"Paul got the highest mark on the test!" the science teacher declared, waving my red checked paper in the air as she came to hand it to me.

My sense of self was as solid as the Popeye cigarettes my parents would buy me whenever I scored a goal in hockey. I felt that I was cast as the right character for this theater-in-the-round on Earth. I suffered disappointments and downfalls like any other child, but I instinctively knew how to handle them. I felt safe.

Until the move.

What set me apart from others in one place was the same thing that set me apart from others in another, but with different reactions. Being book smart and small of frame made for easy pickings in a classroom where everyone, including the girls, already had facial hair, stood half a foot above me and carried with them an edge of anger. It was a simple act to toss me around; to take my lunch; to punch me when teachers were out of sight, or as I travelled to and from school; and to spit in my hair. With great marks came being a marked target. Physically I was at school, but emotionally and mentally I was remarkably absent.

I grew smaller that year. I hid in the crooks of the building. I found different routes to school, even when it doubled my walking time. My voice shrank, my smile eased away and my head hung lower. My once free spirit was being put through an extruder and coming out in an unrecognizable form. The worst part was that I wasn't able to control anybody's reaction. This would be a source of frustration long into my adulthood. I felt splayed out, like Prometheus chained to a rock, whose liver was pecked out daily by an eagle. Livers are renowned for regenerating, and even though I tried to rebuild my spirit I knew exactly what pain would come my way. I was still surprised by how much it hurt.

* * *

"You have a beautiful soul," my teacher said, her eyes softening as she pointed to me from the front of the classroom. This was the same teacher who used to yell at me. She would often turn around and swoon me, in Hallmark card–canned sincerity. I didn't know whether I was walking into a lioness' den in the morning or the boudoir setting of a badly scripted film. Either way, it meant that the spotlight was on me, and it was hard to hide behind my own elbows when the light shone on me. This also meant undo attention when the bell rang.

"He's going to be a handsome boy when he grows up, yes?" she asked another teacher, touching me on the top of my head as the students lined up for class.

Shut up. Stop it. I hate you.

I didn't know if I was talking to her or to myself by that point.

Something had begun to unravel within me. The feeling of safety was gone. I had tried to talk to people about it, but I felt hopeless. No relief came and I started to pray for a dull mind so I would no longer stand out. I didn't care that I didn't know about cars, Van Halen or whatever it is that occupied the minds of the giants around me. I just wanted to disappear into the faded and chipped bricks—to liquefy and drain into the patchwork of weeds that surrounded the schoolyard. To nourish *something*. To feel of use. To be seen. To be remarkable, and not a marked target.

I yearned to fade away.

The Dragon's Keeper

He was nowhere to be seen.

I looked around the corner for the tenth time and saw the same thing—an empty hallway. It was lunchtime, and he would be with the other keepers, perhaps lingering with the wizards and sorceresses. But I knew the dragon would be there. I could feel its heat emanating around me. I rubbed my sweaty palms on my shirt and checked one last time. I took out my paper clips, both opened up into long, metal fingers. I crept up to the door. I began to pick the lock like a proper Halfling rogue thief. I'd practiced many times, but this was the first time I would do it during a formal campaign. I heard some footsteps coming down the hall.

Shit.

My fingers continued to move along the grooves of the lock until I found the right spots. I took a quick breath and turned the picks. The handle turned, too.

I was in.

* * *

Starting in a new school bore the usual pitfalls: the chance of being the outcast, the misunderstood one and the weird kid with that weird kid smell—the chance of being alone. Again. And to do it in the last grade, where everyone knew each other since they were five years old, was an even taller order. The Grade 8 students were segregated to the portables—those outdoor shacks with questionable craftsmanship and even dodgier heating. Sitting at the back of the class was my favourite spot, where I was able to blend into the row of coats behind me. I had no one staring at the back of my head, plotting to harm me in some way. I was the sniper at the top of the bell tower.

Our teacher was docile and puffy-cheeked and he wore penny loafers every day. The floors squeaked underneath him whenever he snaked through the room, checking on our work. He was encouraging and he often let me handle projector duty when it came time for movie time. There was symmetry and mechanical beauty in the movement of film from one reel to the other. He always asked me how my gifted program was going and asked me to share anything I learned there with the rest of the class.

I bonded with some boys, namely Adrian and Chris. Our music tastes overlapped and we enjoyed fantasy. I nerded out heavily with Dungeons & Dragons. I relished in creating and controlling whole worlds. I spearheaded campaign after campaign. I mostly played on my own. I dabbled in playing with other guys, but I was too intimidated by their skill and knowledge. I enjoyed the control that I had when I had maps, 20- and 16-sided dice and my dog-eared monster reference guide scattered around my bedroom floor. There was something about rigging tunnels with traps, creating hordes of horrid creatures to vanquish and having a goal that wrapped up things neatly. I craved to control everyone's fates, including my own. It was a way to bring a feeling of leveling out the bumps of my existence. Of playing large in a small venue. Of floating above the chaos and casting spells and judgment upon all those who were beneath me. In my D&D world, everybody was beneath me. It bred a grandiosity that served me well at that time.

Adrian used to take me to the variety store run by an Egyptian family. "The Pyramid," we'd call the cramped and dingy store. There were two arcade games there, and we spent lots of time and quarters on them, trying to get to that next level. I had watched Adrian's gangly, freckled body dance about the front of the machine, trying to physically will the characters on the screen to greater heights. He was part knees and elbows, part wide aviator glasses. The rest of him was nervous energy. He often asked me to act as cover as he stole chocolate bars or candy from the Pyramid. Eventually, he became my cover when it was my turn. The thrill of not getting caught was my first real high. And like a high, it was short lasting and I wanted more and more.

* * *

The stairs leading down to the dragon's keeper's lair was dirty and poorly lit. A torch would have been appropriate in a proper campaign, but I didn't have that, or a flashlight. The smell of soot and exposed concrete hung in the moist air. I tiptoed down the stairs. As a rogue thief of high skill, skulking around unwelcome places came as easily as breathing. I approached the landing and stopped to peek around the door frame. The increased heat coming from the dragon's belly told me I was getting closer. I muttered a quick elvish protection charm and moved along the walls of the short corridor. I knew that there wouldn't be any traps, but I feared that the keeper may have an acolyte in his place. I shortened my breath until I reached the end of the short hall. I could hear the roaring of the dragon. I was near.

And that's when I heard it.

***

Scoffing sweets was one of many things that the gang took pride in. Ken and one or two other guys joined our ragtag club and soon enough other activities started to crop up: watching Ken's older brother's bad porn (awkward with a bunch of prepubescent boys), throwing snowballs at cars, picking on other kids and causing school property damage. It was seamless in progression. While I had seemed to find my new tribe, there was something in me that chafed at these things. I felt crooked. While I luxuriated in feeling like I belonged to something, I was aching to right myself and centre myself back, before I lost myself.

I had become the guy that I feared the year before. I was the troublemaker. I was the tormentor, the cocksure agitator. I was doing to others what had been done to me and I was propagating the abuse cycle. I felt a perverse sense of power. I thrived in distorted self-will, something that would later mark my life with long-lasting lashes of self-flagellation and collateral damage. But I couldn't release myself from the feeling that I was playing necromancer—I was creating a new life from a lifeless corpse.

I started to create a new life outside of my friends. I struck out on my own. I started to shoplift at different stores, started small fires in corners of alleyways to watch them burn out and see if anyone would catch me and sometimes spied on the teachers at lunchtime to see where they went. I cased the school out. I wandered into places I shouldn't have, like the church next door, exploring their hallways and touching the sacred items to see if they would explode in my wicked hands. I wanted to push my luck until someone stomped on me. The last place I wanted to hit was the janitor's office. The keeper of the dragon. I wanted to see that furnace room and grab something. I didn't know what, but I wanted an amulet, a souvenir, a reminder that I would no longer be told where to go and what to do. I needed to display my *power*.

* * *

The sound of the keeper could be heard at the top of the stairs. The creak of the door clarified the muffled voice.

"Hold on Tony–I gotta check on something," I heard the keeper yell.

I scanned the area for a hiding spot. There was none. I had to push forward.

At least I knew it was safe to go ahead. I slipped into the dragon's keeper's lair. It was much smaller than I had anticipated. It was no larger than a classroom. The dragon was in the corner, breathing gently. It may have been asleep. The fire could be felt, but not seen. Scattered about were assorted tools, chairs and rusted metal pieces that I couldn't identify. A newspaper was laid out, the page three girl showing off in her bikini, like all the other page three girls before her. Boots. A coat draped over a desk. Machinery. I would find an amulet later. I needed cover.

I heard the keeper take a step, then stop. I took a few shallow breaths.

I started towards a door I spied in the corner. A closet door. Or perhaps a portal to another dimension. I wouldn't know until I got there, if I could make it there without being detected.

The keeper took one more step. I could hear him mumble something to himself. Then, another pause.

"Shit—of course I forgot it in the gym. Idiot," he muttered.

The keeper walked up the steps and I heard the door close.

My shoulders dropped as I exhaled deeply.

I scanned the room one more time, avoiding the sleeping dragon, and picked up a few things: a lock and key (assumed charmed), a broken chain and the page three bikini girl picture. Everything would fit in my pocket. I finally felt like I had something of worth in me, even if it was the ratty lining of my coat pocket. I felt that I had value emanating from within.

It was material value, but it was value nonetheless. It was worth more than what I had felt for some time. I had given myself the gift of feeling worthy enough to find treasures outside of me because there were none within.

I made it back up the stairs and into the sunshine and freedom of the schoolyard.

Hidden

There is nothing as bitter as the taste of self-betrayal. Not even the sharp prick of Centennial hops from an IPA could compare to that bitterness, although the alcohol content sure did help in numbing the sting for a very long time. Pulling away from the things that I loved to do, which brought me fulfillment, tore me into thin strips; it shrouded my heart in disconnectedness. I was playing cloak-and-dagger with my own purpose on this earth, evading the things that brought joy and replacing them with seething resentments and increasing amounts of alcohol and poor decision-making.

It seemed a simple idea: find what makes your soul tap

dance then go out and show the world your best jazz hands. For some time I was able to do that. It was a seamless and easy equation to demonstrate and prove. Then, some new math started to get in the way. New equations popped up and shattered that QED at the end of my early proof:

Being yourself = pain.

Showing your hand = pain.

Opening your heart = pain.

Living to your potential = pain.

What the universe had clearly shown me was that what I thought had always been true was not true at all. I had placed all the money on red and it came up black. Bruise black. The wheel kept spinning and so did my head, trying to figure out what I needed or wanted. All the things that seemed to fall easily into my lap—writing, reading, studying and playing music—were the very things that crippled me when I stepped outside my house. They were rigged with traps. It seemed like my life was a stone in my own shoe.

When I was 15 years old I had my mother take a silly picture of me being playful in a mock-up of a hair metal band. I was decked out in the ridiculous layered outfit that many of those 1980s rockers wore, donning my school tie on my head, sporting cut-off gloves and pretending to mutilate an animal (it was an old stuffie of mine). I made the mistake of showing one or two people at school, who refused to give it back to me and passed it on to some of my tormentors. Fresh ammunition. They attacked me like a new chew toy. I had always felt I was a wise elder in the ways of the world, or the neutral observer. In my new analysis, I was nothing more than a mere hatchling, meat for the larger birds of prey.

No matter how much I tried to pull away from the light of recognition, of love, of blooming, I found myself still attracted to it. Like a cat pawing away at a dancing light on a wall, the glow of being seen for who I was slipped between my fingers. I so desperately wanted to be seen. I wanted others to see that I wasn't this strange, isolated, death metal kid who wrote and drew violent and nasty stuff. I was a boy who was hurting and wanted to be held and told "I see you. You are frightened, but I see you. I know what you can do, and how you can affect others. I SEE YOU." But of course, I would have pushed you away if you had tried to do that. The friction between wanting and not wanting fueled the fire of *lacking*.

While I was partially content to have someone find interest in me, I was partially discontented in being found out. It was like a gazelle wanting to spring forth along the grass and bask in the sun, wanting to showcase the blaze of speed and grace it was given, undeterred by predators waiting to descend. So I dissolved into the pack, unseen, or hid on my own. I couldn't tap into the spirit because it was clouded by mistrust, of others and even myself.

What I really wanted was to shine and not be spat at for doing so. I wanted to do what my heart craved and not be harmed for that. I relished the idea of tilling the soil of my spirit and seeing what tender shoots rose up, rather than salting the earth to avoid the pain of someone hacking away at what grew. That conflict between rising up from that place of authenticity and chopping myself down over and over again was the perfect fertile ground for anger and disillusionment. I felt it through me and it was reflected in my choices and actions. It ran rampant in my detachment and resentments towards others. I raged against the girls who rejected me and who went dancing with the jerks instead. I raged against the teachers who picked the dumb guys in the class to shower with praise. I raged against anyone, anywhere, who didn't hold me up high like a rare chalice, to be cherished and preened over, to be put on a mantle and shown off when company came over for fondue.

I often stared at the short stories, scripts and music demos I created and wondered how many matches it would take to burn them up—paper burned easily, but I wasn't sure about plastic cassette tapes. I thought about my glowing report cards, about the trinkets and certificates that marked my scholastic and sometimes athletic milestones, and wondered about tossing them in the bonfire of my vanity. But what would replace that vacant lot, that apparent me-sized hole? I had no idea. I didn't know how *not* to be me, but I was starting to learn. I was starting to see the value in shying away from the authentic me and being left alone. I would be accepted, or, more correctly, I would not *not* be accepted. I could breathe, even if that breath was not mine but a fraud's. I didn't know how long I could live being my own alter-ego, but it was worth a shot; it was worth feigning interest in being someone I wasn't to avoid the slings and arrows of judgment and bullying.

Little did I know just how damaging this would become.

Folding, Unfolding

The art of origami was something that interested me when I was growing up. There was something about the simple act of folding paper into something complex and greater than the sum of the flaps and pleats that drew me to it. I was enamored by the precision of the creases, the sharpness of the corners and the symmetry of the finished work that lined up with the want and need in me to be exacting and definite in what I did. It didn't matter what the final product was—a fox, a swan, or any other animal. What was most important is that it be perfect. Any bulges, crooks or tears were unwelcome and projects with these imperfections found the bottom of my waste basket.

I took all piles of paper I could get a hold of—leftover newspaper, drawing pad sheets or documents that my parents no longer needed—and I hunched over my bedroom desk trying to replicate the maneuvers from the origami book I borrowed from the library. I went at it with fervor. I felt like Dr. Frankenstein, trying to breathe life into something and hoping to animate the inanimate. I wanted that perfect being. I wanted my creations to be perfect because everything about me felt imperfect. If I could create something that was flawless, somehow it would absolve me of all of my own flaws. I needed to manifest something that I couldn't manifest within myself. I was in search of the surrogate to lay waste to Old Paul. Stupid Paul.

Going to school was an exercise in endurance. It was a slow and methodical dismantling of the boy who once felt he could hold the sun and the moon in his hands. It was like taking down one of the giant elephant-like Mûmakil from the *Lord of the Rings* trilogy, one of many books I loved reading when I was younger. Hundreds of arrows and sword cuts were required to take down the house-sized beasts, and in many ways I felt the stings in my travels from the Shire of my own home to Mordor Elementary.

With every punch and insult, with every indifferent adult and turned back, I felt that I was regressing. It was like the universe was telling me that I was improperly wired. I was Beta in a VHS world. The message sent was that I was bad. Having been called a "pansy" and "faggot" enough times, I started to think that perhaps I was those things. They could have been calling me Korean and I would have eventually believed it. The tag team of people hurting me and an eroding self-esteem started to cripple me emotionally. I started to pray for a car to hit me on the way to school and kill me on the spot. I certainly couldn't kill myself because I was too much of a pansy to do anything like that. I was useless. I couldn't fit in with my tormentors and yet I couldn't be myself. I was in the neutral zone—no-man's land. I was in an empty expanse where pain was doled out as punishment for even drifting there. The friction between disappearing and wanting to be in the light shredded me inside.

"You don't know what a blue movie is? You're a fucking idiot."

Unfold.

"Hey shithead, your lunch was pretty good. You didn't want it anyway, right, faggot?"

Fold.

"I'm gonna be waiting for you later, loser."

Unfold.

Crumple.

This folding and unfolding wasn't anything I'd seen in that library book. The creases were blunt and worn, the paper was faded and crumpled and the corners were yielding and limp. What was supposed to be a glorious crane started to devolve into a crippled mutt. What I didn't understand then was that I was as perfect as I needed to be. Imperfectly perfect, like those misshapen origami creations I tossed away. There was still something to be said about their innate beauty, uniqueness and individuality.

I started to feel that perfection was the only way I could ever feel good about myself. It was a futile and hopeless cause, this perfectionism. It was like trying to capture a shadow with a net. But I tried. Every night I tried to find perfection through paper. Every day, I tried to create the me that I was supposed to be. Every time I took to the stack of paper on my desk, I was on a quest to rebuild the universe—a universe where I fit in. I folded until my eyes hurt, my fingers were cramped and there was cosmic dust everywhere.

The Score

They owe me.

This was my mantra as I jacked open the music room door.

They deserve this.

The room had the smell that I always loved—a combination of 30-year-old, musty music books, carpet damp from spit valves and dragged-in snow and a metallic tinge from exposed brass and percussion instruments. There was also the lingering odour of testosterone and Drakkar Noir.

I moved to the corner of the room where I had stashed the amplifier underneath some boxes. It wasn't too big, but large enough that walking out of there with it made it a brazen act.

I didn't need it, but I wanted it, and I was slowly learning that it was always easier to take what I wanted rather than what I needed. My needs were irrelevant to others, so they were to me, as well.

Fuck with me and I'll fuck with you.

The gods of passive-aggressiveness would be appeased that day.

I hustled the amplifier out of the room and down the stairs. School had let out over an hour ago. Most of the other boys would be either heading home or milling about the subway station, talking shit about one another. The rest would be panting outside the nearby girls' school, trying to conceal erections and attempting to convince girls to ride the streetcar home with them.

I didn't have a car, nor an accomplice with a car, so it was a very simple plan: carry the damned thing down a hill covered in slush, unseen, and take the public transit home.

Foolproof. Or perhaps foolhardy.

* * *

It would be a clean slate, this "new school" thing.

In high school, I could surround myself around guys who knew nothing, or at least very little, about me. I could be baptized, reborn and washed clean of my past. I could reinvent myself, play a new role and get tough. Now, it could have been tough to be tough when I chose the flute as my instrument in music class, but many of the other boys played too. I found it was a breeze to be in the woodwind section, because no one could pick on me when I was one of the gang.

I partially resurrected myself in Grade 9. I had to adjust to the fact that, like grade school, the ruling majority was Italian. But not just any kind of Italian: they were what we called "Ginos." Ginos were proud to be Ginos. They had teased 1980s hair, sculpted with the finest of aerosol gels. They wore bangles. Their maroon Catholic school uniform jackets hung over their shoulders, held there with perhaps even more hair gel and sheer will.

I was called a "worm" like some of the other Grade 9's, a sort of hazing that also involved being pushed back and forth in the hallways until your socks and shoes were on one side and your books on the other. I was able to perform my scholastic work without intense scrutiny or physical harm and managed to get an average in the 90s. I thought that perhaps things were turning around and that I would live a so-called normal life. I would find a girlfriend, get a car and maybe go to a reputable university. I had acquired acquaintances at school and I even knew some guys I could call friends. What a coup. The arc of my life's story was rising.

I even smiled in my high school yearbook photo.

Then Grade 10 happened.

***

I took many rests. My arms were sore. I thought swearing would somehow add meat to my muscles, but that didn't work. I struggled to keep the amplifier out of the slush. I shambled and slid down the hill. I was sweating in the late winter, not so much from my exertions but from the thrill of my crime. Or, perhaps it was guilt and anxiety which drenched my white, collared shirt.

I made it to the bus and found a seat in the back. The school's name was spray-painted on the black cover, so I draped my jacket over it; it's better to be exposed to the cold air on the bus than exposed as a criminal. I hoped that the Duran Duran blasting from my Walkman would drown out the thoughts of what I had done. As the bus got closer to my stop, I vowed to let go of that feeling of guilt and compartmentalize it. As I made my way off of the bus, I thought about the sweet music I'd pump out of that amplifier, loud and rapturous. I'd drum those guilty feelings out of my head with some heavy B-flats and G-sharps.

***

"Look, Puller is here."

Tony was with a few of his Gino friends. They arranged themselves like the Jets from West Side Story, but played by

Mario and Luigi look-alikes. These guys could grow moustaches in an afternoon.

The music room was next door to the gymnasium. A collection of extra gym equipment was piled up by the music room door, including tattered blue mats—a lot of mats. I always waited anxiously around this room. I didn't want to get there too early, nor did I want to be late. Getting there early meant getting hurt.

"What's up, Puller? Oh wait, I don't wanna know."

Puller was the name I was christened with at school just after Grade 10 started. I was absent one day because I was sick, and my friends had spread a rumour that my mother caught me masturbating and took me to a psychiatrist. How the rumour gained traction, I never knew. But it stuck. Puller. Paul the Puller.

I looked at my music book. The best thing to do was to not engage.

"Hey Puller—how many times you jerk off today? Do you use your fucking flute to help?" Tony taunted, approaching me. "You know, I always wanted to try something."

He ripped the flute case out of my hand, put me on his shoulders like he was about to do squats at the gym, and spun me around a few times. He paused, then dropped me onto the single mat beneath us.

"Booyah…Bitch!"

The Mario Gang laughed and patted Tony on the shoulder. A job well done, it would seem.

My arm was sore and my head hurt.

I got up just as the door to the music room opened. Wrestling practice was over.

Mr. Sandowski, his shirt collar already moist with neck sweat, asked if I was okay.

"I'm fine," I said as I brushed my nerdy, parted-to-the-left, newscaster hair back in place. I had already learned that speaking to the teachers and guidance counsellors at the school availed nothing. I was on my own.

* * *

Playing the flute was more than just putting my fingers on the right pads, possessing good aperture and keeping time. It was a passageway for me. It transported me away from the shots I absorbed outside the music room. It was a cradle. I rocked back and forth like a metronome and swung on the notes. It kept the anger docile. It temporarily smothered the pain.

I was good at the flute. Very good. I was taking private lessons on the side, and there was something about making music rather than just reading notes off a page that spoke to me and stirred my soul. I loved how the notes on the page told a story. Quarter notes, trills, arpeggios—these all mapped out a journey and a destination. The notes on the page were set, perfectly arranged. They had a cadence, a rhythm and a force that I was missing in my own life. The scores were generous with rests, but other times furious flights threatened to carve right into the book itself. It was my job to find the heartbeat on the page.

I also played the tenor saxophone. I didn't have the same passion for it as I did for the flute, but it was music, and it also let me be in the jazz band. I was able to perform several times during concerts. I was confident in these concerts. I felt I found my space when I performed in front of others. There was a soloist every year, and the best player in the class was often asked to be the soloist. I knew that I was good enough to be selected. I could feel it. I would finally be seen for the talented guy I was. People would see me differently. I would be accepted. I would be in the spotlight.

"Mr. Sandowski, I wanted to know if there is a chance I could be the soloist this year," I asked one day after class.

Mr. Sandowski was at the podium, arranging his books. He dabbed at his moist neck and took his glasses off.

"Paul, you're an amazing player. You have a gift."

"Thank you, sir," I said, gripping onto my flute case.

"But, this year, Matt is doing it. And next year, Jordan is

doing it because he's staying an extra year. I think Donny will be the year after that just because it's his last year. If it weren't for that…" his voice trailed off.

"What about if I stay another year? Do you think—"

"You're much better than those guys, and you know that, but it's because of the way it's arranged. I don't see it happening. I'm sorry. But I know you have a future in this." He inhaled deeply and scratched his chin. He forced a smile.

I left the room. I didn't want to play the fucking flute any more.

* * *

The amplifier did the job; it made my poor bass guitar playing louder. Unlike the flute, the bass was nothing to be embarrassed about. From what I could gleam from the ratty rock band posters taped to my bedroom walls, bass players got chicks. Well, mostly the singers and lead guitar players got the girls. Drummers and bass players got the leftovers. It was a moot point, as I didn't play the bass as much as I imitated someone who plays the bass, but it kept my monkey mind occupied. It kept me from thinking about school, about what a loser I was and about how I was a disappointment. If my life until that point was a made-for-TV movie, the scene where I snag the most unlikely hot girlfriend with a heart of gold would come soon after the next commercial and things would smooth out.

The problem with the amp was that it solved nothing. The initial elation of getting the new shiny object wore out quickly, and I was left with me once again. My soul felt as discordant as the notes I wrenched out of the guitar. The guilt started to weigh heavily on me. I couldn't look at the amplifier without thinking about how I desecrated the one place at school that I felt at ease with myself. It was the one place where I was seen, where I was acknowledged because of skill, not reputation. None of my nighttime blood-soaked revenge fantasies occurred in the music room.

I stared at my flute case, untouched for days, in the corner. I looked at the amplifier.

Shit.

I unplugged my guitar, wrapped the amplifier in a garbage bag and put it by my backpack for school the next day. I opened my flute case, put together the instrument, and played a tune. I can't remember what it was called, but it was easily memorized.

Fuck school.

I knew the score.

Cerveza, Por Favor

My first real drink happened on a dull day, in a dreary month, at a drab intersection, in a dismal part of town. This wasn't sucking on the foam of my dad's can of beer after opening it for him. This wasn't watered down *vino rosso* at the grown-ups' table or an experimental sip of something that seemed interesting and daring at the same time. This was a premeditated guzzle of warm beer with my drinking cohorts. Someone's brother—I think most people's drinking adventures start with "someone's brother" of whom there should be a vague statue erected from crushed cans—bought for us a case of beer. We did what most people do when they get a case of beer; we took it to a faded, grassy median in a dilapidated part of town and drank it there, surrounded by the car exhaust and ennui, attempting to look cool.

Many alcoholics will tell you that the first drink they ever had felt like mother's milk, and that is was like sucking at the teat of bliss. Many will describe that feeling as warmth, as coming home, or as hitting an inside-the-park home run. Most will describe to you that sense of completion, like knowing that they had found their soulmate. But I could not say that about my first drink. My initial thoughts were, "This doesn't suck too much."

Adrian, my lanky friend from grade school, was in many ways the leader of our group of castoffs. Property damage was his specialty. He had a lot of misplaced energy and even more unfocused anger. This was when he was sober. Add a few beers to that 150-pound frame and he upgraded to more destructive and risky behaviours. We often felt compelled to go along, for fear of his teasing. For a bunch of limp-tailed wusses who lived their lives at the losing end of taunting tongues, being bitched at by one of our own was even worse, like getting slapped by your younger sister's friend.

"I have to work tomorrow. And I'm not feeling that good," I told Adrian, loud enough so that the other guys could hear me. I could sense that the others weren't up to anything other than just chilling.

"Fuck that. We have shit to do," Adrian said, throwing a rock at the back of a yield sign a couple of metres away. "Besides, we still have all this beer to drink."

I looked at the beer. It didn't call out to me. Bed did, though. And I still had a long ride home. "I'm going. You guys can dick around here if you want."

I turned around and started to walk towards the bus stop. I could hear the guys joining in on Adrian's jokes. Their laughing blended into the traffic noises whirling around me, as the two beers I had had turned my brain into an echo chamber. I felt tired. I shuffled away. I felt no upward rush, no delirious sense of grandiosity or invincibility—just a touch less like *me*, and bit more neutral. I didn't mind it, but it wasn't something that I craved to do again soon. I didn't see the use of it.

I crossed the street and breathed in the foggy air, stared at the apartment complexes around me and waited for the Birchmount bus to take me to the subway station.

***

"You coming to the party tonight?"

Dale was flipping through his order pad, keeping an eye on the kitchen pass, where the finished plates would eventually be.

"I don't think so. I just want to go home and chill after work," I said, leaning on my mop.

"What?" Dale asked, leaning in closer.

Dale was a compact man, short, wide and with a low centre of gravity that gave him the gait of a woolly mammoth.

The clinking of plates, the whoosh of *tostones* hitting the deep fryer and the hood exhaust fan in the kitchen made quiet casual conversation difficult.

"I said no, Dale." I walked over to unload the rack of dishes that just finished its cycle in the machine.

"Why not? We're all going," Dale said, following me. "Just come for a few beers. A *cerveza* won't kill you."

"I have beer at home if I want," I said, stacking the dinner plates.

"Well, so do I. That's not the point."

The sound of a bell snapped in the air. Food was ready. Dale shuffled back to the pass to pick up his order. The smell of refried beans, tortillas and cilantro was strong but comforting. I worked at the restaurant only on weekends, but I always loved the smells that came from the kitchen. The cooks often let me help them prep by peeling onions, stirring sauces and chopping jalapeños. I played with ingredients I had never heard of or tasted before.

"Look, just come for a bit. No biggie. Just have one beer. One," Dale said as he lined the plates up his arm. He started to head to the dining room. "I'll give you the address later."

I stared at my feet. Why did they want me to go? I didn't know these people well. They were just as inviting and friendly as a game show theme song, but that's because they were at work: they got paid to be nice. I didn't understand why they would want me around. I was used to people pushing me away rather than inviting me closer, especially when I smelled of garlic, detergent and poor decision-making. Maybe I would go for one beer. That would get them off my back. Just one.

"Yo, Paulie. Dishes, man…running low here!" one of the cooks yelled at me.

I grabbed a stack and hustled over.

Just one beer.

* * *

I rode my bike down to the house, cradling a six-pack—the quintessential Canadian care package of gatherings. I arrived at the semi-detached house in about fifteen minutes. The front yard, if one could call it that, was festooned with tacky dollar-store statues, garden gnomes and even a bird bath. They choked out all but a few blades of grass.

I stood at the door, wondering if I had made a mistake. I could be at home, cocooned in my bedroom, mucking around with my computer, listening to Slayer and planning revolutions in my head. My hands were sweaty. I cleared my throat, as if I were trying to dislodge my unease. I opened the door and walked in. People were grouped up in twos and threes, chatting. Vague music coated the room. Voices and laughs cascaded about. Arms flailed as tall tales were no doubt being told. People ducked in and out of doorways, replenishing drinks. They all seemed to fit together, these people. They had a sense of belonging; they clicked and whirred like a Swiss watch. I felt like a clumsy, misshapen cuckoo clock.

"Paul! You made it! I didn't think you'd make it, ya bastard," Dale called from the other side of the room. I gave him a furtive smile to recognize his comment.

"Beers are in the fridge. Make yourself comfortable." Dale took a long pull from his bottle of cider, crossed his arms and fell back into his conversation with the manager of the restaurant, who was still wearing his tie.

I made it to the fridge. The cramped kitchen was littered with bottles of all shapes and sizes. Clear liquids, murky liquids, liquids spilled on the counter top. I obeyed Dale's request and grabbed a beer for myself. I looked around at how people clutched their drinks, wielding them like scepters. There seemed to be a power held within those glasses, those vials of majesty.

I drank my beer. I sat on a chair by a hutch. I stared at the floor, memorizing people's shoes and laces. I finished my beer. There, it was done. I wanted to show Dale that I was finished, like I would show my mother that my plate was clean of the weary vegetables she heaped on it. I wanted Dale to see I fulfilled my promise, then I could hop on my bike and head home. But there was something about the room, the lighting and the vibe that shifted—it grew slightly softer, more inviting. Everyone appeared less judgmental, their stances more open and their laughter more welcoming.

I took a deep breath, inhaling it all in. I took another breath and walked towards the kitchen. Jerome, one of the cooks from the restaurant, was there. He was a hulking man. When I watched him work on the line he enveloped the space, all pots and pans danced in his hands, yet he was deft. The knife seemed to sing in his grip. He was quiet, but he had a laugh that carried through to the dining room.

"Paulie, good to see ya! Glad you didn't chicken shit out of this," Jerome said, reaching over someone to pat me on the back. He was surrounded by a few people I didn't recognize. He towered over them. They looked like planets orbiting the sun.

"Yeah, well, Dale said that—"

"Where's your drink? Did you drive?"

"Uh, no. Well, yeah, my bike is—"

"Goddamn, let me get you something."

Jerome moved away from the solar system of bodies and went behind the makeshift bar beside the sink. He poured me a drink. I asked him what it was.

"Rum and coke, bud. Cheers!" He touched my glass with his. He took a long swig.

I stared at my drink. I'd never had rum before. It smelled like disinfectant. Sweet disinfectant.

"Cheers," I said, quietly. I took a sip. It felt like vinegar scraping against my tongue, but I continued to drink it. It went down quickly. I made myself another one and drank it, leaning against the kitchen counter. I started to smile at people. I began to feel my feet and fingers come alive. I walked back into the living room with a fresh drink, trying not to spill it. I noticed how the room just glowed with humanity and goodness. I wanted to dive in and roll around in this feeling. I felt the energy of the room enter my bloodstream as easily as the Appletons did. I wanted to talk to people, but I didn't know what to say. I didn't know how to do it. But I wanted to join in to be connected for once. I wanted someone to talk to me because they wanted to, not because they felt obliged to. I wanted to talk to actual grown-ups who weren't guidance counsellors, teachers or my parents. Actual people.

The night was a psychedelic swirl of sounds, textures and sights: a hand on the shoulder here, a riotous laugh there, a stained shirt somewhere in the mix. My feet left the ground and I was whirling about on an axis I never knew existed. I was free of me. I don't know how long I was there, but at the end all I remember is trying to ride my bike home. It was futile, and the scrapes and cuts were adding up. I recall arguing with a taxi driver about how to put my bike in the back trunk.

I sneaked into my house—something that I would do with regularity for years to come—and haphazardly landed on my bed. The room spun. I felt ill. I felt alone. I felt as if my "good" me, the "real" me was left behind somewhere in that front yard bird bath, leaking onto the ground next to a pile of Pilsner-induced puke.

As I lay on the bed, one foot on the ground to stop the spinning, I regretted drinking so much rum. Why didn't I just have that one beer and call it a night? It felt good to feel good, but the price to pay at the end was too rich for me. I didn't enjoy feeling like a chew toy who just went one hour with Brutus the Pit Bull. I wanted off this ride.

But it did feel good while it lasted.

I had arrived.

Anger – Forgiveness

"Bitterness is like cancer. It eats upon the host. But anger is like fire. It burns it all clean."
~ **Maya Angelou**

"Forgiveness does not change the past, but it does enlarge the future."
~ **Paul Boese**

Semifreddo and the Art of Digging Two Graves

"Before you embark on a journey of revenge, dig two graves."
~ **Confucius**

Revenge. The word just rolls off the tongue, gliding effortlessly in a deep growl, gladdening the dark heart and appeasing all senses. It's a word to wallow in, to drink from with both hands cupped, brought up to parched lips. It conjures up images of scorned women on daytime soaps, of karate apprentices honouring murdered masters and of countless gang drive-by murders. It is drama and anger, twisted up like the stripes on a candy cane, as cold as semifreddo. Dangerous ground for a cat like me.

I had always viewed myself as a laid-back guy. Chill McMellow. Nothing seemed to bother me. I was like The Dude in *The Big Lebowski*, just lounging about, letting everything and everyone slip off of me. But of course, it was all a façade. I may have been hanging easy on the outside, but inside I was shredded up with insecurities, fear and Titanic-loads of anger. But I denied that I was an angry person. I'd never gotten into a fist fight or harmed anyone physically, so how could I be angry?

Many people have calming thoughts or routines before slumbering, such as a rundown of the day, a guided meditation in their ears or just a rolling lull that passes through them as they close their eyes. For me, it was fantasies. Revenge fantasies. There were disembowelments, beheadings, shooting sprees and plenty of slow, painful deaths. My thoughts before the onset of sleep resembled a video compendium of torture porn. I felt comfort immersed in this blood sport; it was like a security blanket knitted from sacrificial lamb's wool. The horror scenes were the only way I could find sleep. I didn't slash people up in real life, but I certainly cut them down with my words. I impaled them with my sarcasm and superiority. I carved them up with passive-aggressive actions.

My mind ramped up all emotions and reactions by a level or two. Or ten. So what I call "anger" many would call rage. "Dislike" to me is what the average person describes as pure hate. My "liking" something is another person's obsession. When I talk about fear most call it abject terror. What I refer to as exacting some degree of revenge is what a stiff off of the street would describe as complete and utter obliteration of that person from the face of the planet.

Hey, at least I wasn't an *angry* guy. The Dude, remember. Abiding like a fucker.

My journey of revenge involved digging those proverbial two graves on a daily, almost hourly, basis. My arms were sore from picking up that shovel, yet I couldn't put it down. Just like booze. My days were spent like Madam Defarge, knitting her hit list and slowly but surely cultivating her hate. Knit one, snarl two. There was no end to the carnage that played out in the abattoir of my mind.

The problem was, of course, that I didn't exact revenge at all, in a mafia-type sense. But I did drink *at* people, drinking the poison and hoping they would die. It was a poor tactic, but it made sense to me at the time. My heart was eaten alive with hatred, my mind was saturated with animosity and hostility, and my soul was weighed down with resentment. I dripped venom from all pores, yet I carried a sandwich board with "All Is Good" scrawled in blood and wine. I was imprisoned by my own anger. The acid I tossed about splattered me as well.

It was in recovery when I started to see and understand where all of this anger stemmed from: my expectations of myself and others, my lack of self-love and self-worth, the seeking of validation from externals, my shortage of forgiveness towards myself and others, and the overall lack of connection to the Creator. I was angry at myself for being weak, for being useless and for being less than a man (however I measured that). I couldn't see that I was who I was created to be, and that loving myself and accepting myself could bring me to a place of peace. I couldn't see that I was a child of God and not one of His rejects in the runt pile. There are no rejects in His world. I couldn't see what others saw in me. I only saw what I wasn't.

A person who hates themself can only hate others. When there is no room for love within, there can be no love extended without. I felt that as I started to accept and (gulp) like myself, I found my capacity to accept and like others grew at an equal, if not greater, rate. I can only reflect what is within. When I saw garbage, everything and everyone else was rubbish. Once I was able to cultivate and harvest self-love, I was able to love others. It's an act that still continues today. I still succumb to my old ways at times, but I know I can return to the garden if I choose.

It's been some time since I have luxuriated in revenge fantasies. I don't have the need to get back at anyone because I try to leave all anger at the door. When I find myself disturbed, I quickly examine why (*What am I fearful of?*), acknowledge the reason and move on. I don't give unhealthy anger room to breathe or breed. I don't have that need to hurt others by choking out my spirit anymore. Years ago, I could have told you how many bullets in the chamber I needed to fulfill my revenge plots. I would have also added an extra bullet to that total for myself. But those days are over. There is peace where there wasn't before.

I have put the shovel down.

Disservice with a Smile

I was never a fighter. I have never known the sensation of hitting another person, knocking out a tooth or feeling someone's jawbone crack beneath my knuckles. I have never had to roundhouse kick my way out of a predicament nor body slam someone because of a perceived slight ("He was dissing me...with his *eyes*"). When fists came flying my way, my roster of defensive moves were limited to turtling or running away in a cowardly fashion. If I were in school, hiding behind the nearest teacher was—to me—an acceptable coverage maneuver. While I didn't know how to use nunchucks, there was one weapon I could wield with sufficient force and precise motion; I had one weapon that no one could wrestle out of my hands or swipe from my locker: my words.

As I moved past high school and into the drifting ether of skipped university classes, dodgy job choices and pub-crawling solo through Europe, my one constant companion was the written word—mine and others. Books and journals fell out of my backpacks as easily as quotes stumbled out of my mouth. Words were my mental and emotional failsafe when things crumbled around me. I learned to harness words in forceful ways as needed. I found that a sharp tongue was as bruising as an elbow to the forehead or kick to the lower spine. The venom of a snake is what kills, not the bite. I recognized that when I was forced into a corner, language deflected, disarmed and disabled others. I didn't require the psychic discipline and physical prowess to manhandle someone in a tight situation; I just needed a fistful of well-chosen nouns and verbs tied to resentment. Like honing a machete against a whetstone, my tongue was sharpened on the abrasions left by my anger. Liquid courage didn't hurt either.

My first foray into the dark arts of sarcasm and other verbal jab jobs was rough. I had no real mentor or master to help me along, so I figured it out on my own, although hanging out at bars and knowing a lot of smartasses helped. I learned to defend myself with cutting remarks and abrasive verbal assaults. I could suit up in stealth mode and cut people down without leaving a mark. I could come off as being polite and caring, and yet I was peeling strips of skin off with a glad and earnest look on my face, my intonation high and full of mock enthusiasm. It was a private joke that only I understood, and it made me feel that I had a voice and a sense of power.

This wasn't simple vulgarity—that was reserved for the plebes and dull of mind, don't you know. For a so-called gifted child, I needed to operate at a higher level. I wouldn't allow myself to be brought down to Neanderthal-grade anger, where the savages attacked one another with hairy fists. Sarcasm was the weapon of the *intelligentsia*. I was able to sit on the emperor's throne above the melee and drop my displeasure like tiny bombs, safe from the shrapnel and blood.

At least, that is what I thought.

The fact was that my anger was at maximum drive, just dressed up in a tuxedo rather than in wrestler's tights. It was a deeper, more lingering anger. Many of the guys who used me as an unwilling sparring partner hit me because they could. It was primal, instinctive stuff. The anger that lined my inner landscape was beyond punches. It was without an outlet. It was pent up gas in a canister that was ready to crack. Words were the only way I could keep it from ripping me apart from within. But the same words which seemed to save me also wounded me in the end, just like alcohol did in the long run.

When I used my words as a scimitar, I was also slicing away at my own authentic self. I was playing a role. I was Atilla the Hun, Lord Voldemort and Basil Fawlty blended into a frothy façade. When I cut at someone, I also cut into myself. I picked at my resentments and low self-worth like a scab. I created an environment of toxicity. I was coming from a place of fear rather than a place of love. My "wins" were tainted by self-inflicted wounds.

Part of my process of growth has been learning how to deal with anger in healthy ways. Lashing out like Leviathan is ego-gratifying and feels good for a moment, but it leaves a mark, and boo-boos need to be kissed. Being angry in itself is not a character flaw—there are times when speaking up or being assertive is necessary. Learning how to harness anger in positive ways is the real battle. Understand that there is a dimmer switch when it comes to anger; it doesn't have to be at 11 at all times.

The words I speak to others is a reflection of where I am with myself. When I spat venom, with a smile or not, I was showing my hand. My fractured inner landscape was being splattered on the canvas ground. I was wrapped up in hurt, with ego and pride as festive bows. When I am kinder to myself, my words soften, my approach relaxes and my intentions mature. It takes practice to harvest my actions from that place. It's not the automatic "you are here" sign on a mall directory. I often need to peg myself there early in the day so that I am square to the day and to the Creator.

I know I have made progress because I find that when I do allow myself to come from that dark and angry spot, I feel uncomfortable. It's no longer something that fits me, like it used to. These aren't those high school jeans which once fell over slender hips. It's a tight squeeze and it sucks the breath out of me. So the simple and kind thing is to speak from a place of love, acceptance and gratitude.

It's true service with a smile.

Fair's Fare

I saw those guys every day.

I waited for the bus at the station, exhausted from my 12-hour work day. When the bus finally pulled in, people snuck in off the street, using the salt-stained vehicle as a cover, running into the station as if they were a part of the other fare-paying customer corral coming off of the bus.

Heathens! Malcontents! Artichokes! Phylloxera! Iconoclasts! (Apologies to Captain Haddock.) What angered me was that it was just so *unfair*.

Why should I have to pay while those cats get to just stroll in, unencumbered by the weight of paying for their ride? Why do I feel like such a schmuck standing here, allowing them to freely break the law? Does it even matter? It isn't fair, is it, Paulie?

Well, of course it wasn't. News flash: Life isn't fair. Huh? But everyone knows this, or is supposed to know. I am just getting this. Just. Now. About thirty-five years too late. This is something that was taught to me in grade school, but I was probably in the little boy's room when that part of the lesson was handed out.

The idea that people of material wealth, fame and entitlement could treat people poorly and somehow be adored by so many and then die not knowing the pain they brought upon others was a notion that brought me grief. At the same time, I felt that so many beautiful, generous and kind people would live in poverty- and violence-laden lives to die alone, perhaps under savage conditions, and no one would notice their shine. It was a black-and-white, almost militant view I held on to for a very long time. It kept my undefined rage engaged.

The idea of life being unfair was bolstered by my need to play victim. I could hang my hat on the anger that I dished out like playing cards on poker night. If life was unfair then instead of changing it I could at least bitch about it. It was much easier than tackling problems like an adult. Now, when I look at the big picture, the idea of life being "unfair" or "fair" is matched evenly by how I view gratitude and the perspective it gives me.

When I think about how things are unfair to me (and it's almost always about me, of course), I lose sight of the big picture; I lose sight of where I stand in the grand scheme of things. When I get into the sickly head space of "Why, why, why me?" I am blocking the light of things that are already serving me. Life will be unfair. I don't say that with a sneer or a ton of irony (unlike the Starbucks barista making your latte this morning), but in a matter-of-fact way. I say it in a way that actually brings me to a place of acceptance.

When I feel that things are unfair to me, what I am really saying is that I am more deserving than others for some things. I am putting myself and my needs above others. It says that I know best in regards to what people should and should not get. It harbours envy and other malicious ways of thinking. When I look at someone and point and cry out "Unfair!" I am really speaking out of wounded pride and ego.

So what does "fair" look like then?

There is no real thing as "fair." There are similar words, such as "just," "equitable," "unbiased," "neutral" or "nonpartisan." They shed their own light in more specific ways, but in terms of what people "deserve," that's a cheesecake of a different flavour. What's fair to me isn't fair to you. So I can only focus on myself, the only thing I can change in my realm of being. (Note: I am not talking about social justice or anything like that, where societal consciousness can be influenced by healthy resistance and other ways of protest and declarations of change. I am not talking about corporations raking in millions while children starve to death in unbearable conditions. This is about things on a more personal level.)

So what about that co-worker who steals your ideas as their own and gets a raise or promotion because of that? What about the sleazy roommate of yours who gets the girl you've had your eye on for a while? Unfair, isn't it? Yeah, it is. But who's to say that these things weren't meant to be? Perhaps it isn't luck or fairness at play here, but instead this is what those people need so that they can grow in some way. We often grow most when we are in tough or uncomfortable situations. While it may seem that some folks have "won" the day with their ill-found booty, who's to say that they aren't struggling in a way that we don't see? It comes down to perception.

I used to rail against people who coasted through life, prospering off of others and taking advantage of others. I work hard for what I have, so how fair is that? That's how I used to think. I don't fly off the handle much anymore when I encounter coasters. Why? It's because I see that they, like everyone else on this planet, are fueled by fears. They may not even know they are afraid, but they are. Perhaps that is the only way they know how to be. Perhaps they aren't being malicious after all, but just unaware. So who am I to judge? I have inflicted a lot of clueless, malicious and unintentional damage in my past. I have coasted through life myself at times, drinking, self-pitying and mooching. Spiritually, I was on the edge of the sidewalk, cap in hand, working an angle.

Have I been completely honest throughout my life? Not at all. Have I taken what is not mine at some points? Absolutely. Have I been a cheat, a liar and a thief? Yes, yes and yes. Have I walked away from situations where I should have been horse-whipped and shown to all as an example? Indeed. So who am I to tell others what is best for them? Who am I to say what is "fair" and what isn't? I've had my share of hoodwinking others, emotionally scamming them. So being the judge of other people's lives is hypocritical.

Perspective is what keeps the overreactive ego at bay. Understanding that it's really none of my business what happens to others allows me to walk away with a certain detachment that keeps me in a more peaceful place. Sure, I still might find myself annoyed, but it's a far cry from the unhealthy and debilitating resentments that used to keep me frozen in my mind. Perspective frees me from the bondage of self and allows me to see things from a different point of view.

As for those people who sneak onto the subway, I am sure

they aren't happy to be doing it. I am sure they are full of fear of getting caught, fear of being judged by others (like me) and fear of being embarrassed. I am sure that if they need to cheat the transit system, they probably need the money more than the company does. A guy at work once admitted to me that sometimes has to sneak onto the train because he can't afford the $6 each day. I don't judge him, and I don't lecture him. It's his deal, not mine. He knows it's wrong, and he feels bad, but that is where he is right now in his life. Who can honestly say that they would never resort to that? Anyone? Bueller? Bueller?

When I feel that I am getting the short end of the stick, it's usually because my perspective is warped or I am not seeing the opportunity for growth, love and acceptance. Acceptance is the key. Acceptance and perspective give me the tools to see things in a different light, to lighten the emotional load and to come at things in a new way. I may not "like" it, but I learn to let things go and eventually I experience things with greater clarity, which helps me later down the line.

Fairness is a concept, and hence not often a reality. My mind can barely deal with the minutiae of my day, let alone lofty ideals such as what is best for me or others. Simplicity is the key to serenity, and so I keep my side of the street clean.

That's a fair statement.

Ones and Zeroes

Binary code. So what does that have to do with your latte? Nothing, except that the barista ringing in your order used a computer register, and computer registers, like all other computers, use binary code (unless you go to a shop that embraces the abacus still and employs a posse of howler monkeys in the back to smash coffee beans against rocks, which would be fantastic).

Binary code is a system of 1s and 0s. Every computer language and instruction boils down to binary code. It's all that computer processors understand. 1 or 0. On or off. String a few of those bad boys together in the right order and you're on the road to programming the next *Halo* sequel, teaching a robot to weld bolts to an aircraft carrier or using Wikipedia to cheat on your essays. It's the bare bones basic code for all machines.

I'm no computer (yet—the Borg are still a possible threat), but I identify with the 1s and 0s in a way. There is that old tale of going to a party or large gathering and being told by 99 people that you're great, you're wonderful and you're a pleasure to be around. But there is that one person who doesn't care much for you. You know that one? The person who, for whatever reason, just dislikes you or doesn't make you feel welcome? Guess who would leave an impression on me after I left the building? The One. In my drinking days, I collected Ones like I collected empties.

Throughout my life, I stored these Ones like a memory card or computer chip. I let them embed themselves into my consciousness. They became a part of me, and they never got dusty because I constantly pulled them out for inspection and polishing. Holding those Ones in me became automatic. I resented these people, I worried about what I had done to have them not like me and I tried to figure out what I had done wrong. I wanted them all to just love and adore me. But it wasn't to be, so I hated them. I called them names and whistled the *Kill Bill* tune while I did atrocious deeds to them in my mind. Most of all, I cherished them because without those Ones I was nothing. I was a Zero.

This collection of mine was borne out of countless fears and resentments. They were the protective film that kept those Ones fresh and away from the daylight of rational thought and emotional maturity. This cherishment held me back from developing on an emotional and spiritual level. It cut any progress I may have had down at the knees and still asked me to get up and dance. I despised this collection and yet I clutched onto it and let it absorb into my cellular structure. And the more places I ventured out to, the more of these Ones I picked up.

As I collected more and more of these Ones, the sicker I got in my alcoholism. Work, public transit, neighbours, store clerks, imaginary beings—these were more foot soldiers to add to the battalion that hacked at me all day and night. I fed them with my ill thoughts, my unwavering attention and my obsession over them. I brought them to life every time I put them on trial, when I kicked up the emotions behind the resentments and played the tape over and over and over and over again. I cradled them like delicate eggs.

And the Zeros? Start at self-esteem, self-worth and self-value. Continue down the aisle and experience the vacancy on the shelves of self-love, compassion and empathy towards others. Circle around and comb deep to find empty vats of serenity, contentedness and peace. I had Zeros abound, and I got used to them.

So I hunted and gathered these Ones, and I nestled them amongst the Zeros. I arranged them like notes on a newly composed sonata. I designed a new code every time I got out there and threw myself under life's wheels. I programmed myself to feel and to not feel. I programmed myself to stay chained to a bottle that I didn't want and yet craved. I programmed myself to be less than and yet greater than, to stay self-contained and yet wanting out.

The funny thing with having such a dangerous collection as mine was just how much capacity I had for the Ones and Zeros in my life. I felt that I was boundless in terms of how much I could endure. The resentments and fears buoyed my illness and kept everything negative and harmful afloat, while sinking what few positive and dear things that may have made the mistake of coming up for air. There was no plan of action when it all started. But like the mythical and theoretical perpetual motion machine, it seemed to put out more energy than I was putting into it, and it spun out of control.

Frankly, I might as well have been a machine. I felt empty inside, with not even a fan to cool things down. Booze tried to cool me down, but it got into the gunk and it jammed me up worse. Booze became another set of Ones and Zeros processed and caked onto the motherboard, with no IT dudes to fix things up. I didn't have a clue about what could help reset my system.

In the end, there is truly only one One which I need with me at all time. In *The Big Book of Alcoholics Anonymous*, there is a section that reads "Remember that we deal with alcohol-cunning, baffling, powerful! Without help it is too much for us. But there is One who has all power—that One is God. May you find Him now!" It wasn't until my system burned out and crashed that I was able to see this. My Ones were just garbage and clutter. They kept me focused on the wrong things, and drove me deeper into self and self-absorption, selfishness and anger. In turn, they helped to create new code for my alcoholism to read like old punch cards. Archaic, dodo-like stuff. Defrag material.

Today, I get to shake those Ones out before they accumulate. I have learned to let go, to detach, and to not take things personally. I have also learned to show compassion and love, to have tolerance, to help others, and to have communion with the Creator. When I do get a stowaway in the old cranium, I have ways of extracting it: I delve deeper through inventory, I talk it out with someone or I meditate upon it until I find the answer to what is disturbing me.

I have a new hard drive. I have a softer heart. I have a new One. I have new Zeros. The Creator has hit the big reset button on me, and I am ever so grateful for it.

Selfishness – Generosity

"Selfishness comes from poverty in the heart, from the belief that love is not abundant."
~ Don Miguel Ruiz

"A heart that gives, gathers."
~ Tao Te Ching

The Window Played to the Scene of Me

I had never lived in a basement apartment until then. I was newly separated, and only seeing my wife and young son once or so a week. I had no job, so my days consisted of 12-step meetings, looking for work and trying not to drink. I rode on a perpetual roller coaster; one minute I wanted to hug everyone on the street, the next minute I wanted to strangle them. There were days I hated meetings, hated the people in the meetings and hated recovery. I hated myself. I hated me for me and I sometimes wished I didn't have to deal with me any more—sober or drunk. It was like living on a Mobius strip where I couldn't live with drinking and I couldn't live without drinking; I existed on both sides of the paper and yet not on it at all.

If you had asked me how I was doing during those days, I would have shot you a smirk and cried out, "Living the dream!" I may have punctuated it with a noogie or Celtic jig. Perhaps I would have given you a brotherly punch on the shoulder.

About two months into my still minty-fresh recovery, I was taking the bus to an early morning meeting. I sat on my favourite seat—left side single seat, beside the big central window. Loner's Corner. The bus was about a block or two away from the terminal station and was in queue to make a left turn. Traffic held us in that line for a while. As I sat waiting, I had this overwhelming, unexpected and astonishingly firm resolution that I would commit suicide at the subway station. Just like that. Suicide. The Final Sacrifice.

I didn't think of my wife and my young boy in that very moment; I was self-absorbed in the pain of not being able to live the way I was, or not thinking I could. Ending my life in a horrific and absolute way only seemed fitting and logical. My family would be better off without me, without having to deal with Ol' Alkie Paul. There would be no more need to check in on me or worry about my state of mind. Sure, there would be overdue library fines to deal with and closets to be cleaned, but short-term annoyance would yield a longer lasting sigh of relief.

They say that suicide is a selfish act. I would argue that it's a desperate human response to pain that is overwhelming and voracious. I was so wrapped up in my own darkness that there was no room for the light of rational thought. My state of mind became warped. I truly could not see a life worth living when my one and only way of coping had been removed from me. Everything stung at the lightest touch. I saw the final, definite knot at the end of the unraveling thread of my existence.

As I walked off the bus and down the stairs to the subway platforms, something shifted in me. The want and need to step in front of one of the rushing trains dissipated. It was if my mind was hijacked with some sense of grace long enough for me to make it down to my meeting, where I was still shaking with fear and copious amounts of strong coffee. I confessed my suicidal thoughts that morning to a group of strangers. Some nodded their heads or patted each other's backs as I shared. A few people came up to me afterwards and told me that they, too, had similar thoughts in their journey. I would have to take care of my own library fines for the time being.

The next day, I was on the same bus route, heading to the same subway station. I sat in the same seat, by the same big central window. The bus was in the same place, stopped and waiting to make that same left turn. Traffic held us in once again. Outside the window was a bright blue sky blanketing a church. About six feet from me a casket was being hoisted into the back of a hearse. Family members wailed and flailed, smacking the palm of their hands with their fists, as children watched, blank faced and wide-eyed. I looked at the casket. I pictured myself in it. I saw my wife's face on one of the women curled up on the sidewalk, legs splayed out like a newborn foal, wearing yellow heels. I saw my son's face planted on the little boy wearing a tie that was too tight, not knowing why he had to dress up nicely only to see other nicely dressed people cry. I felt the heat from that moment in my skin. I held on to the pain that the scene was painted in. I wanted to hold on just a little bit longer, but the bus pulled away.

Six months later, I was living back at home. I was back in the big bed. I had done a lot of work in my recovery. I still wasn't where I wanted to be, but I certainly was far from where I didn't want to be. I had made some progress, and the mental obsession had been lifted. Alcohol wasn't on the menu for me anymore, and I was on the mend. My emotions had started to even out. I felt like I was almost normal — whatever that meant. I had hope. I had something possible going for me, and I was starting to just *be* instead of running away from me.

After a day at my new job, I was on a bus going home. I sat in Loner's Corner. It was snowy and overcast out, and the windows were caked with salt, grime and frost. I couldn't see anything out those windows. The bus was waiting to make a left turn. Traffic held us in that line for a while. As we waited, I caught a small movement on the window beside me. Someone was drawing a happy face from outside of the bus. A simple happy face, looking at me. Just as the smile swoop of the face left the person's finger, the bus was on its way out.

I watched this happy face, seemingly random in its time and place, and thought about my journey of recovery. Faith and love and God had taken me there. That window had catalogued me in two short scenes over many months. One had shown me the darkness that could come from light, and the light that could come from darkness. I was shown that there are outcomes, choices and ways of being. I felt the power in both scenes. I felt The Power.

The window played host to the scene of me.

Keys to the Vault

Work has always been fertile ground for my alcoholism to grow and prosper. I work in an industry where alcohol and drugs run like tap water, where a 14-hour shift is considered the norm and where personalities clash like stripes and plaid on a polka dot skirt. I work in an industry where bravado and machismo run the roost and where weeding out the weak is a spectator sport. The hospitality industry is notorious for its neurotic and egotistical notables who push the limits on creativity and ambition, and often that drive carries forth into general debauchery and mischief. Did I already mention the copious amounts of alcohol and drugs?

As a hospitality manager, I was often bestowed with one great honour: the keys to the liquor room. You know, just in case one of those in the lower castes wanted to pinch a bottle of the "good stuff." I was trusted with keys. To liquor. Handing an alcoholic the keys to the booze vault is like handing an alcoholic the keys to the booze vault. Learning when to and when not to use those keys was a bell curve for me—an inverted bell curve filled with Sauvignon Blanc and shame.

I could indulge under the guise of work-related functions and tasks, and no one would really question my state. I could sneak in a few soul-easing shots of whatever was nearby. If it was in an open bottle, it was fair game. As long as I could get my job done, I was rarely taken to task about my behaviour. It's a part of the culture I work in, and I had maxed out that card. Remember, I had keys.

Of course, like all good alcoholics, I went too far. Uneven efforts, calling in sick more often, running late—these all began to concern some people. I was not one of those people. Policy changes were made because of me. My key holding status was often revoked. I was no longer asked back to places I used to be welcome. No one said anything, but I heard what wasn't being said loud and clear. My alcoholism was affecting my work considerably, to the point of being unemployable. Cue the depression and further anxiety, and fuel that with more booze.

I was keyless and clueless. And drunk.

As an adult, I had always defined myself by what I was, where I worked and who I worked under. I measured my pedigree against those of others. I waved my CV, and smugness, like a samurai sword, and felt self-righteous in my judgments of others. At the same time, I felt blank and unworthy inside. But regardless of how I was within, I could always count on my title and rank to give the illusion of confidence. If I was cornered at a party, at least I could talk about my job. It was safe, but it also gave me a sense of being human-like. Alcohol took all that away from me, and as the shine seemed to fade from my career and reputation I felt ineffectuality stirring. I was feeling as hollow and useless as one of the empties I hid in the kitchen recycling bins.

The feeling of usefulness is inherently strong in humans. No one likes to feel useless, and I had sunk into that deep dark well of being unable to perform or be of service to anyone, including myself. It wasn't until I started to heal that I was able to grasp some very simple truths. First, I am more than a job description. I am not the *job*, but a *someone* who holds a job. I am not a robot. I am also replaceable (take that, ego). Second, my value as a person doesn't come from what I produce at work or from what title is printed on my business card. I exchange services for pay. I do my best to do what I am asked to do and I often go above and beyond that because that is in my nature. There may be "bad" workers, but there aren't "bad" people. Third, I can be of service to others at work in non-work related ways. I can offer people a shoulder to unburden themselves. I can bring co-workers coffee or treats. I can cheer someone up. I can make a new employee more at ease by giving them encouragement. Work is not a place without emotions and sensibilities.

At work, I am able to practice principles in my professional affairs. I get to practice creating and sticking to boundaries. I get to practice spiritual principles. I get to do things for others outside of my usual tasks and objectives. I get to practice patience. I have talents and skills that were God-given, and I get to use them properly. I have a healthy pride in my work and I have passion again. I actually enjoy what I do, even though it can be challenging at times, and that breeds consistency. Work for me is almost like a walking meditation, at times, because the act of being physical lends itself to mindfulness. I feel useful in all senses of the word, and that helps fill up my self-esteem tank, where I once tried to power myself on the fumes of booze and inadequacy.

What I do to make money is my living, but my real job is being true to myself and being of service to others. My work life and my spiritual life aren't two separate entities. If I was able to look at the landscape of work as a place of fueling my anxieties and resentments, I can also look at work as a place to replenish my spirit and energy. Work is not always fun, and it can add certain stresses, but knowing that I can always take time out to pray or to access my higher self and seek answers is a way that I can maneuver through the day. This is a practice I will take with me wherever I go.

In that regard, I will always have the keys to a greater treasure.

Can't Talk Now I'm Putting my Halo in with the Delicates

I always had this image of myself as a selfless man—a real Johnny-Do-Good. "Oy, here's a six-pence, mate. Go fetch a gosling for your goodly wife." I did all the cleaning, cooking and grunt work of the house. I made sure that I kept a tidy home and a decent looking exterior (I am not a gardener, but I know a weed when I see one). I always sacrificed my time and energy to let my wife and others do what they wanted while I took care of the kids (mine and others), ran errands or just took on stuff so that they could go out and enjoy life. I felt that I rarely got asked what my needs were or what I wanted to do. I watched whatever shows or movies people wanted to watch, let others take the best piece of lasagna and I acquiesced to the general population. I was pretty damned selfless, wasn't I? A man of good standing? Of charity and loyalty? Didn't I exude a whiff of, shall I say, sainthood? Perhaps it was no coincidence my name was Paul — biblical royalty.

It was all lies.

During those times, deep down, I was an angry, resentful, lonely, and broken man with no self-esteem. I was selfish and self-centred. I played martyr and victim. I thought I was totally selfless when at times I was really making everything about me. "Poor Paul, works too hard," "Oh, Poor Paul, look at him sacrifice himself so much," "What a guy, never asks anything in return," etc. This act of throwing myself on the sword was my way of seeking approval and attention. I was passive-aggressive most times, which screamed of anger, and I took digs at people in the kindest, gentlest ways without them even knowing I was digging my talons into them. I cursed all those on my grudge list, usually while muttering in the laundry room. If you had heard my rumblings and asked me what was going on I would have cheerfully extolled the virtues of the new detergent I bought that week ("It's in cube form; it takes the guess work out of free pouring, guys!"). I was never honest. My alcoholism fed off this form of neo-narcissistic dodgeball.

I began to recognize this behaviour once I started my work in recovery. It was a challenge to open my eyes to the idea that Saint Paul wasn't so holy after all. I had to rewrite the Testament According to Me. In my work, it was suggested that I wasn't as snow white as I made myself out to be. ("How dare you! Do you see the shine on those floors? How about those stubborn grass stains gone from the kids' jeans? I work hard so you don't have to.")

I came to understand that I had no boundaries; I allowed people to treat me the way they did because I treated myself the same way, and they saw that I was fine with that. I had a perverse sense of control when I played the martyr. I nailed myself to a pressure-treated wooden beam because I felt better than you while I made myself less than you. I also took offense to things. Deep down, I wanted (and expected) pats on the back, applause and the occasional parade when I should have been doing what I did out of love, service, purpose and humility, rather than for critical acclaim. When I didn't get what I wanted, I pouted, threw another load of clothes in the laundry and hauled another resentment onto the pile. Lather, rinse, repeat.

Coming off of the high of Hallowed Be My Own Name was not easy. I still sometimes find myself detaching from the ground and floating up like a lazy balloon, but I can often snag myself on a tree limb before I get too far up. These days, I offer myself in service to those who accept it, and I also accept service extended to me. I am leveling myself to others in my realm. I no longer placate the parts of me which want to play God and determine who I am better than or less than. I've had to look and examine my motives for everything I do. Is it out of love or applause? Is it ego-driven? I have to sort these things out sometimes, just as I sort out the clothes in the hamper. I learn to separate my authentic self from my prideful self. I adjust my boundaries. I square myself to the world. I check my intentions, play true to myself and deal with moments when I want to put that halo back on.

Eventually it all comes out in the wash.

Deception – Honesty

"The ingenuity of self-deception is inexhaustible."
~ **Hannah Moore**

"An honest man lives not to the world, but to himself."
~ **Wellins Calcott**

Myth Busting with a Rocket Launcher

"**I** don't ride in snow. Period."

I declared this statement countless times. It was a pat answer to when someone asked about my winter riding habits. Most people who know me know about my almost fanatical attachment to bike riding. It's my main mode of transportation. I ride daily, and that includes winter. No matter how cold it is, I will ride. Temperature isn't something that will cause me to wipe out. "Cold" doesn't need shoveling or plowing. Cold is a state of mind, and if my state of mind is right, I can ride through sub-Arctic climates. When my mind is not right, a random gentle breeze on a summer's eve might send me off shivering. But ride in snow? Nope. Not this groovy, dry cat.

For years, I dared not traverse in the fluffy white stuff because I feared wiping out or falling under a bus. It's happened before, hasn't it? Nothing I could cite, per se, but in my mind I am just sure that it's happened. It must be on the internet somewhere. My mind knows even when it doesn't, *capisci*? That is how the ego and the justification/rationalization of my mushy mind rolls. But the fact remains that I had no direct experience with riding in snow. So why the mental block?

I lived much of my life under the default position of "I can't do that." No matter what it was or how difficult or easy it may have been, it would seem that I was genetically incapable of giving anything an honest college try. Unless it involved me getting more drinks in me. Then sure, anything goes. Self-seeking is a gas, man. It's the same with opinions: I venerated my own opinions regardless of annoying roadblocks like facts, experience or evidence. There seems to have been a hard line set in the embryonic stage of my (under)development. This border that had stormtroopers all over it, falling prey to Jedi mind tricks. Even when things were possible, the line remained firm.

When I set my mind to something, it's as good as gold. Regardless of the veracity of the thought, it sets and sits like concrete. "Knitting's for old women," "Rock climbing is dangerous," "Meatloaf (both the singer and the dinner) looks like dog food." Blanket statements fall from my mouth like icicles off of skyscrapers under the sun. While some of what I think and feel is borne out of true direct and indirect experience, much of what sticks to me has no basis. This sounds a bit, you know, presumptuous. I close my mind to any other possibilities. And a closed mind, like a small room with a paint-shut window, remains stale and bereft of light.

Being unbending and keeping a cool distance from judgment keeps me barricaded against the Creator's plan for me. It keeps me crushed under the stone of ego. It keeps me in the ref's chair above the tennis match of life, with a blindfold on, yet still judging wildly. It darkens the areas of my life which require light to survive. Even small statements like, "I don't like Mexican food," to the bigger, "I hate all foreign cars," to even, "I will never get sober. Guys like me were meant to die young," can close my mind off easily. In all of these cases, it's a matter of answering back, "Says you." Huh? Have you tried every single Mexican dish? Or are you basing that statement on a bad burrito from Taco Bell, which is about as Mexican as a Smurf is a space shuttle? Have you driven every

Volkswagen, Porsche, Audi, etc. on the planet? Have you ever tried a recovery program with complete honesty and willingness?

Those are the kind of verdicts that pass through me all the time. "Says you" is my way of telling my lower self that it is having an opinion that is based on nothing but fear, laziness or the unwillingness to reach out and try something new. "Says you" is that husky voice that demands me to delve in a bit deeper and substantiate my claim. No ticket, no ride, buster. Get into the back of the line and try again to get on the Pile Driver Water Slide.

When I make blanket statements that really may not be true, am I being dishonest? Am I being judgmental? Am I being selfish or fearful, too? Of course those play a part. I often need to examine myself for any knots that I'm tying up inside. I need to determine if I am stating a passing opinion or a matter-of-fact truth. There is nothing wrong with having an opinion, of course. We have opinions. Opinions can be strong, mild or plain, just like chicken wings. I just have to ask myself where they come from and if they are authentic to me.

When I am not authentic, I get fuzzy in the mind and crusty in the soul. I get twisted up mentally and spiritually. I am not centred and I feel off. I have had my share of off, thank you very much, so I will do my best to stay centred. So what I try to do is keep my opinions on the up and up. I keep exaggeration and hyperbole low or non-existent. I fly straight. I minimize the boastful and prideful. I stay open to other's opinions. (Whoa, who said that?) I leave room after my meal for the dessert of appeal and discourse. I prepare to be wrong. I do some investigating before I flap my gums or strike keys on the board. I invoke empathy. All of these things are intertwined into serenity.

When I keep an open mind, I keep open the endless possibilities of not only being wrong, but of the growth that comes with that. I keep open the chances to find new passions and loves. I keep open the chances of getting deeper into a new phase of life. I keep open the avenues of exploration, fun, balance and excitement. I am giving myself a chance to live in a new now, a new normal and a new playground. I get to see that being right does not mean being happy. I am ripping apart at the old stories and old truths.

It's all about personal myth-busting. With a rocket launcher.

As for bike riding in the snow, I took a chance one day. I gave my fears a left hook and traversed in the aftermath of a moderate snowfall. I didn't go ass-over-teakettle. I didn't nearly slip under a vehicle. I took my time and enjoyed the sound of the snow crunching underneath my tires. There is a type of quiet when the world's babble gets absorbed into the downfall, a quiet that brings things into focus.

I guess I do ride in snow, after all.

I'm Fine (I Want to Die)

How many times did I utter this phrase, knowing that approximately 99.9% of the time I was far from fine? If you could find a map of the universe (eBay may have one), plunk "Fine" down in one random spot, calculate (don't forget pi) and circle the polar opposite, that's precisely where I would have been. Without a doubt, I would have either had my head down in a toilet bowl, retching up the regret of the night before, or had my head up my ass in denial about what a disaster my life was.

The ability to cover up is a skill that I learned early in my drinking days. I would assert that I learned it even before I picked up a drink. Of course, active alcoholics haven't cornered the market on "fine" (ask any parent who has a teenager), but we certainly rely on it much more than we should. Learning to cover myself and my true feelings through the fabrication of a false bill of goods was a necessary habit. Letting people in on how I truly felt often turned into a betrayal or a dismissing gesture. I felt that I was burdening others with my troubles, so even when I was shredded up inside and torn to bits, I was "fine" when asked how things were.

Fine indeed.

There is a time and place to reveal the ticking time bomb within, of course. When the crossing guard drops the whistle from their lips and asks, "How ya doing, pal?" I'll do the polite social contract thing and say something positive yet non-committal like "Good" or "Fabulous. How about that local sports team?" There is an expectation that the question is more of a kind consideration or hello than an inquisition into my emotional state. Done. Easy. It's the other stuff that's hard.

When I was drinking, thinking of drinking or recovering from drinking (which combined took about 95% of my daily time), my emotional landscape was full of craggy rocks, sharp stalagmites and bogs of self-pity. Add a healthy dose of anxiety, teen angst poetry-like depression and resentments up and down the place and you had about as un-fine a wonderland as you can construct. Like Dollywood, but built by Goths. On quicksand. What do you say to someone when, deep down, you feel like a Bergman film scored by Nick Cave, Leonard Cohen and Connie Francis? It's easier to gloss over the pain than acknowledge it. It's easier to take a pass than meet the hurt head on. Why open the vault, when tightening the locking mechanism seems much more effective?

A part of me felt that by saying I was OK when really I was collapsing under the weight of my own darkness I would perhaps be able to trick myself into feeling fine. Perhaps if I gave that tepid word enough energy, it would manifest itself into a meager smile, or at least get me away from the fire of my own pain. "Fake it until you make it!" they say. Faking was easy. Telling you I was alright was a way to keep you away from me and to bolster the little one-act passion play I had going on inside. I could crucify myself over and over but I'd only let you see the setting sun behind the hill and not the nails and cross. I played into my own fantasy that I wasn't important enough to be fretted over by anyone, including myself.

So it wasn't until I couldn't hold back anymore, when I was brimming with enough toxic "un-fine-ness," that I broke down. Binges, anxiety attacks, lashings of self-pity, angry diatribes—these all played out to a sense of doom and failure. The dishonesty and shame of going against my own grain only fueled things further. I wanted to let the release valve go, to just be held and told that I would be OK. But I didn't share with others because I didn't want to look weak or foolish. How damning that was to myself. How cruel that was. How selfish towards those who would have been able to help, people who were itching to see my pain go away.

"I'm Fine."

Part of my alcoholism was fuelled by the denial of many things: my drinking problem, the emotions and conditions that preceded the drinking and my mental state. In dealing with the booze issue, I've had to make a big turn on accessing my emotions. Where I would once be blank, or overwhelmed, I have had to learn to not catastrophize everything, to not let things take over or to let go of a lot. Honesty had to be implanted and cultivated. Allowing others to help and to allow my pain to get into the open and to be worked with was new to me. I had to learn that it was fine to tell someone that I wasn't feeling fine, that I felt like drinking, that I hated myself and that life sucked.

And guess what? The earth kept revolving. No one died. I was able to not vent, per se, but to engage in a dialogue with my hidden self, the one I tried to smother with my "fines." I was able to see that negative feelings are still feelings, and they carry as much weight as I want them to. It's alright to feel good and to even admit it.

I was picking up my sons the other day from across the street where they were playing with the neighbourhood boys, and while I was getting my kids ready the mother of the boys asked me how I was doing. I blurted out, "Wonderful!" The mother and father looked at each other and then back at me. "Wonderful?" Yes, wonderful. I joked about perhaps having my Oprah voice on or something. But I was feeling wonderful, and didn't want to devalue or dismiss that feeling. Just as if I wasn't feeling fantastic, I would acknowledge that too, without getting maudlin or morose.

There is a power and force that comes from true honesty and direct contact with the emotions that burble, bubble and squeak beneath and over the surface of my spirit. I am not perfect in this. I am still learning to trust where I am in the Fine–Un-fine spectrum. I can gauge my internal temperature and know that it is neither good nor bad, but just is. Lying about it only disarms me, and I can't be there fully. I spent enough of my life not being fully there. While learning to balance the true sense of me, having a healthy emotional identity and creating a false self is a delicate thing.

It's a fine line.

Changing History

Imagine being able to change history. Your history. Of course, we know we can't change the events of the past — those are a done deal. The future — that is fraught with uncertainty. It unfolds underneath us and can be shifted and morphed by our actions and behaviours, but often the externals of the world press upon us and put things into our path that we are powerless to change. An ill loved one, an unexpected letter, an emergency, a promotion at work, a new person walks into our life, etc. — these are things that often catch us off guard and have to be responded to in an appropriate way. The present, depending on your view of the present, is either now, gone and happened in the instant we are in it, or we can make the incremental and hummingbird-like adjustments as we move throughout the day. Turn left instead of right. Answer the phone or don't. Decide to react angrily rather than out of love and tolerance. The present is a stream that is broken into staccato semiquavers that play out as the moment flows to the next.

So then, how does one change history? Look back to the past, I say. Yes, the same past whose events cannot be given a cosmic mulligan. Or is it so cast in stone that there is no wiggle room of any kind? Is there a way of changing the past through the motions of the present? Is there a way of resetting some of the pain and hurt? At the risk of coming off like a snake oil salesman, yes.

Sort of.

When my first son was born, it was a life-changing event for me. I was now a father—no longer a reckless hack at life. At least that is what I thought at the time. I remember the evening that I brought my son and my wife back home from the hospital. It was cold outside and I fumbled with the car seat buckles. Anxious and unsure of what to do with this newborn, I was careful in lifting him into the house. My wife went to our bedroom to rest, so I was left with my little boy. Alone. Eyes open yet closed, he ensnared my spirit and heart with his vulnerability, with his energy, and with the simple fact that he'd just been transported to yet another new place in his young life. He was ours. He had been removed from the cherished spiritual world and brought into the material. I cradled and rocked this boy, this wee soul. As we both looked at one another—he through dim light, I through a mist of tears of both joy and of melancholy—I swore to him and to myself that I would never drink again. Ever. I told myself that that was the moment I would end my drinking career. It would mark my early retirement.

This never happened, of course. The insidious nature of my alcoholism pushed away even the most sacred of this love and trust, crashed through the bond of blood and engaged my bloated ego to pick up the bottle again. I gained an engorged liver to match my engorged self-righteousness and pride. I continued to promise myself and my son that today would be the last day. And then the next today. And the today that followed the upcoming week. I was unable to stop, regardless of the greatest thing to happen to me in my fractured life. Even the emergence of a little child could not break the chains of my alcoholism. I couldn't stop drinking and I couldn't stop being the old me, even for the sake of this beautiful and innocent boy. I prayed nightly for my sobriety, even as I railed against God for bringing this poor baby to a wretched father like me. What did this little angel do to deserve a pathetic excuse for a father and human like me? Damn you, God.

You can say that is a part of my story. A small part. A painful part. There is nothing I can do to take back the fact that I drank while this little child was in my life. I wasn't fully present for him, or anyone for that fact. And it got worse after that…much worse. For years, I carried this history in my back pocket, like a worn handkerchief. I stared at it often, resenting myself, regretting moment after moment, playing it all over in my head day after day like a spool trapped in a loop.

If you were to look further into that back pocket, you would find my one calling card—the only card in the deck, in fact. It's a good enough deck for solitaire, but lousy for poker (you could say, though, I had the "crazy" part of Crazy Eights and the "gin" part of Gin Rummy down pat). There was one word embossed on that card: "victim." That, too, was my history, my story. I was a victim of bullying, I was a victim of circumstances and I was a victim when it came to other people. Oh, such sorrow! Everything in my life boiled down to being a victim and then feeling the after effects long after the victimization. And on and on it went, carved into granulite with the chisel of resentment.

We all have had our stories. We still do. Old stories, told over and over again in our minds, spilled out to anyone at the bar who would listen and spat out whenever we feel we are further wronged. New chapters are added as they come up.

Our stories focus more on those who wronged us and less on what our part was. Our stories are blurred and stained by anger, fear, worry and spite. Our stories, seemingly set in kilned clay, adapt to our inner landscape. They help to separate us from others, to show us that we are different and that no one can ever understand us. Divided even further from our true selves, our stories dig us deeper into a place where the darkness fosters even more darkness.

So is that end of the tale, then? Do I sit in the mindset that the past is just that and I can't do anything about it? I saw things as being permanent. I thought my stories were obelisks to mark the failures of my life. A psalm song from the Book of Loser, in the minor key of jackass. What I have learned is that I *do* get to change the past. Not the actions, per se—they are fossilized for social studies students to study and archive at their whim. But the magic remains in how I change the *perspective* of the past. I get to shift the old reality into a new reality. I get to change history—my history—as I know it.

Self-forgiveness showed me that I was not only freed from how I felt about my old transgressions, but I was also freed from the shackles of the sense of failure that I had had about my life and of my behaviour. I didn't absolve myself of my actions—I still had to take responsibility—but it changed how I looked at myself for all of those years. Working through my inventory and making amends to others also cleaned up a lot of that, too. I no longer needed to carry that victim card. I could also toss out shame, guilt and remorse while I was at it. The cross no longer fit me and it was laid aside to build a garden bed, to allow growth rather than crush it. In doing this, my whole history changed. I didn't feel like the shell of a human anymore. I wasn't a shitty dad. I wasn't a person who was terminally unique and apart from his own light. I saw that I was simply a sick man and a broken spirit. The Creator had never abandoned me. I was the one who was blocked off from Him.

This reminds me of one place that I used to work at—a place where I was very active in my alcoholism. My co-workers there were pleasant enough to me, but I felt that they treated me in a way that I didn't deserve (paging pride and ego!). I felt that they pitied me, that they didn't take me seriously and that I was just a burden to them. I truly believed that they just tolerated me, that they were all against me and that they pretended to like me because they had to. I felt alone, disgruntled and angry. I stamped that victim ticket over and over like a coffee shop points card, except the only reward I received was more isolation, resentment and self-pity. I eventually quit that place, and while they took me out for a goodbye dinner and said kind things, I still felt like I was nothing to them. Now, that used to be my story. If you had asked me even a year or so into my sobriety about that time in my life, I would have spun a lovely yarn where I was David facing Goliath.

Here is where history changes.

When I went back to make my amends to two of the people at that place of work, this is what I found out: they had been very worried about me when I worked there—about my drinking issues. They had checked with the Human Resources department to ask if there was anything they could do for me. They had been afraid to talk to me about what was going on with me. They had turned many a blind eye to my behaviour because they knew something was wrong with me and didn't want to see me go. They had discussed among themselves what they could do to help me. They had done all they could to include me and make me feel like a part of the team because they sensed I felt different. They had cared about me like I had not seen in such a long time. Upon hearing this, my heart lifted, my soul soared and history changed for me. My story had completely changed. The facts remained in many ways, but the complexion and hues were different. When I tell the story now, I look at my part, where I was acting like a jerk, where I was unreliable as a co-worker and employee and where I was not present or useful. I see what it was like through their eyes. I am not a victim, nor a villain. I am just a player in a scene, and now I see it with fresh eyes and an unburdened spirit.

There are many places that my history has changed: how my parents raised me, how I grew up, how my school life was, etc. All has changed as I continue trudging the path with eyes open and awareness intact. My old life, while still rocky in places, is set on a different foundation now. My old ideas and perceptions continue to shift and glide the more I uncover and peel back the layers of myself and grow in my spiritual journey. I am not a victim. I can be victimized at times, but I am not a victim. The common denominator in my life, good and bad, is me. So how do I look back and interpret the past? How do I want to see it and how much of that is truth? It's an ongoing process, and while I am not looking to sanitize the past or gaze longingly on it, I am aware of where I have come from and how I choose to see it.

While I am able to occasionally drift back and see things with a new pair of glasses, it's the present that matters. The choices that I make, the counsel that I take, the communion with the Creator and others I seek, the continued challenge in growing and learning—these are the things which allow me to expand into my new life. These are the lessons I can pass on to others. These are the tools I use to erase and smash the old conceptions of me and slowly unveil the me that I was created to be, the one where light shines strongest. We all have that light.

More shall be revealed. Let others bask in your light.

A Scattering of Dubious Intentions

Intentions. Motives. Expectations.

These get as easily entwined as headphone cords. It has been said that the world judges us by our actions, not our intentions. As an alcoholic, my intentions were wonderful—Nobel Prize–winning doozies, dolled up in lace and hard-won Jazzercise sweat. My intentions could be etched in carbon or burned onto titanium, preserved for later generations to study and reflect on. But really, when put up against the light of my (in)actions, my intentions might as well have been crafted on an Etch A Sketch during an earthquake. My intentions truly were dubious and shady. More specifically, my underlying motives were the dodgy dogs. The added expectations that came from my intentions and actions created resentment, and resentment is a monster truck that loved to rip into the soil of my serenity.

In my deep heart of hearts, when I set out to do something, I really did mean I would set out to do something. The thought was concrete. The intention was solid and unwavering. Whether I followed through with the action was beside the point. I already gave myself brownie points for thinking about thinking about doing something, so in many ways it was a *fait accompli*. It was already scrawled into the record books. The ledgers of kindness were bursting.

Here's an example of how I would manipulate intent: I invited my mother to a home-cooked meal at my house. So I made the call to have my mother come to the house for dinner (after delaying it, making excuses, etc.). So far so good. Now, my motives for treating my mother to dinner? That's what I examine next. I wanted to be selfless. I wanted to be a good son. I wanted to pay a little bit back for all of the wonderful meals she had made me. I wanted to see her smile. But I was an active alcoholic, and my motives were rarely that clean. Really, what I wanted was to look good (because I didn't have much self-esteem), to have an excuse to go to the liquor store (all foods require wine in the recipes, right?), to feel some love (because I felt unloved), to get compliments on my food (because I didn't value myself in any way) and to look like the martyr (self-pity—I can roll around in that filth all day). See how this was falling apart? My intentions were then self-serving. I was not doing this for mom, I was doing this for me.

So what I did was cover a bad motive with a good motive. I flew with a bomb on board. And like so many times in my life, that bomb went kaboom and scattered shrapnel on a lot of people, with me taking the brunt of the force. It's kamikaze-style self-servitude.

When mom was over, I was slaving over a hot stove, refusing help (martyr) and indulging self-pity (*Oh, they don't know what it's like being me; let's have another splash of wine and quietly chug some vodka on the side for strength*). But I'm a good son, right? Right? (No self-esteem.) These internal conflicts were pushing me more to the drink. But it didn't end there. We ate dinner and I got the compliments I craved ("Divine seared red snapper, Paul."), and then what did I do? I deflected the compliments (not worthy, low self-worth, selfish). Then expectations crept up on me.

Why didn't she compliment me on the potatoes? Why isn't she going on about how I set the table? Why isn't she putting away the plates and cleaning up after me? Why isn't she phoning her friends right now and raving about this dinner that I haphazardly and sloppily put together while trying not to spill my drink?

Then, that bomb gets lit. Expectations morph into resentments and my internal landscape is leveled. My mother, my family, is suddenly selfish. She has no manners. Doesn't she know how much work I put into this?

Intentions. Motives. Expectations.

Multiply this example by 20 or 30. That's what went on every day in my mind. Add the guy that had cut in front of me at the bank. Add the cashier who hadn't said bye to me when I had bid her farewell. Tack on the bus driver who seemed a touch too ironic and snarky for my liking. There was no wonder I drank. No wonder I wanted to get out of my own head. No wonder I pushed down every emotion I had. The expectations I heaped on others, including myself, were like layers of wet clothing pulling me down. No wonder I had a hard time giving people the shirt off of my back; it was soaked with expectations.

Fast forward to today. I am much clearer with my intentions. I am much better at knowing when I am trying to fool myself or others. I stay focused on what it is I am truly trying to achieve. I detach from the results. I don't put expectations on anyone or anything. It doesn't mean that I don't have a certain level of anticipated response towards others (I expect the bus driver to stop at the next bus stop when I ring the bell), but I do my best not to emotionally invest in the actions of others. The act of chopping wood and fetching water is my mantra for the joy of itself, the work. I come to everything and everyone as clean as I can be, motive- and intention-wise. I watch my feet as I take the actions I need to. This sounds easy, but not always easy in practice. I can slink back into that quicksand, that place of getting swallowed up by my own thoughts. I am a work-in-progress.

The reward for making the mental shift is that I don't carry the resentments I used to carry. I am not as disingenuous with my approach. Where I once gave someone the shirt off my back and expected a fur coat in its place, I now expect nothing but a slight chill and the hope that the person is warmer. Do I still carry a bomb with me sometimes? Sure. Intentions are like metal detectors at airports: I have to check my baggage — my motives. If there's a beep, I step back, empty out my expectations and walk back through again.

No beep. No bomb. No boom.

Arrogance – Humility

"Arrogance is a kingdom without a crown."
~ **American Proverb**

"Humility, that low, sweet root, from which all heavenly virtues shoot."
~ **Thomas Moore**

I Don't Have Contempt Prior to Investigation, I Just Don't Like What I Don't Like

It is amazing, the number of ways I can say "no."
When I was drinking, it seemed unfathomable that I could not know things. I was a smart guy. I knew *stuff*—remarkable, funny and brain-blowing stuff. I was learned. My report cards attested to my Mensa-worthy status. (Note: I wasn't anywhere near Mensa-worthy status.) To suggest that perhaps I could learn something or see things in a different light was laughable, nay insulting. I wouldn't say ego was present. I would say ego was Godzilla-like, breathing fire,

stomping on buildings and making people run out onto the streets. Everyone wanted to get away from me. There is nothing worse than a know-it-all who doesn't seem to know very much.

It wasn't so much that I didn't want to admit that I didn't know it all, but rather that I didn't want to admit that I didn't know what I didn't know. I had the warped perception that I was open-minded and receptive to new things, like a young child or a curious scientist. For someone who had taken pride in having a mental and creative playground as vast as the Prairies, I never considered that perhaps it was more as confined as being strapped to a chair. My actions showed me this. If you had started a sentence with, "Hey, you wanna check out—" I would have jumped in with "No."

"I heard there's this really good—"

"No."

"You want to try—"

"Hell no."

I couldn't open myself up to anything outside of the realm of what I knew, and hence what I was comfortable with. The only problem with this is that my world got smaller by the day. The more I drank, the more I denied, the more I lied, the more I feared, the more drama I created and hid from, the more I tried to play God and failed and the smaller my comfort zone became. Still I became more entrenched and staunch in my egotistical and egocentric view that I still had all the answers.

Take that, Prairie Boy.

I shut down people because my own mind was shut down. I didn't want them to see that I was stuck in a place of ego and fear. I couldn't believe that perhaps there was something, anything, that I did not know that could actually be of use to me. If I didn't know about it, it didn't exist. "That might be good for *you*," I might have said with contempt dripping down my chin like melted ice cream, "but that's not for *me*." I was asleep to the fact that I was useless to myself and others. My ego imprisoned me, and pride made sure I stayed there in lockdown.

"There is a principle which is a bar against all information, which is proof against all arguments, and which cannot fail to keep a man in everlasting ignorance — that principle is contempt prior to investigation."

This phrase, found in *The Big Book of Alcoholics Anonymous*, sums everything up for those who suffer from grandiosity and fear. My contempt was fear-based, pure and simple. My everlasting ignorance was disguised as worldliness. My bar was my ego telling me and others that I knew better. I had all of the answers to questions no one was asking. It wasn't until my life finally crumbled into small feta cheese–sized bits (and bits just as stinky) that I had no choice but to step into the big unknown, then into lots of smaller unknowns, then again back into some big enchiladas. And so it has been since. Plunging headlong into things I would have easily dismissed in the past currently happens only because of my connection with God, and trying to follow basic, but life-changing, spiritual principles.

My automatic resistance to things outside of my realm has softened into a willingness to grow, to understand and to embrace. I am more open to hearing things out, to compromise and to take small and large leaps of faith when approached with something new or different. While I am no longer dropping knee-jerk "no"s wherever I step, I am still not yet at the "I'm up for anything" side of the meter. I may not get there, nor is that my goal. My goal is to be flexible, keep an open mind and let things flow through it. I will often catch myself screaming in my head, "No way, Jose!" but I will keep my mouth shut and my ears open. I will quell the rising tide of negativity and swallow it down. I am more able to take in what someone is saying and actually consider it before making a more informed decision. I am not clutching at their jugular before the last syllable has left their tongue.

This radical shift for me has given me new perspective in how I approach life. It opens me up to things that may branch off into other things, and that's the fun part. Life is rarely a straight line from Point A to Point B. I usually detour through dingy tunnels, craggy hills and snarled roundabouts. That's where the interesting things happen. And frankly, Point B is often overrated. It's the journey itself which is best understood felt through the bottoms of my feet, not through mental gymnastics.

I pray every morning that I go into this world with an open heart and an open mind. It's a tall order. Contempt prior to investigation is an old thought, an old way, but still loves to butt into my conversations. It didn't serve me then, and it certainly doesn't serve me now, although it does like to crop up when fear is lurking. But I just pause, mentally skip over the "no" in my mind, and breathe. There is no "yes" or "no" in the moment of the breath. It just is.

More than a Bushel Full of Brains

"A handful of patience is worth more than a bushel of brains."
~ **Dutch Proverb**

When my oldest son was six years old, he received an over-abundance of LEGO for Christmas a few years ago. There is one theme per year, and that year it was all about those little things that I love stepping on in the middle of the night on the way to the bathroom. The sharper and finer, the better. Now, this isn't just a box of random blocks like I had growing up. These are specific, custom kits that require more instruction and documentation than the Treaty of Versailles. Miss one piece the size of a pinhead and the thing doesn't go together properly. A monster truck ends up looking like a stack of wet doilies if not properly put together. This not a Box-O-Imagination. It's construction work on a Lilliputian scale.

The day after Christmas, my son started to put together one of his kits. He constructed it without much parental help, which was a first for him. The major muscle he was flexing and building was his patience. It's a muscle that can quickly atrophy and jump start the occasional meltdown. Watching him was a study in studying, in breathing and in just being with the blocks, one by one. He saw what was needed and followed the directions in the booklet, going back when he made a mistake. Sometimes he had to check in with either me or my wife. But overall, he was able to pass through the tough parts of the build without stomping away like, well, a six-year-old kid, or a middle-aged man who sometimes thinks the world revolves around him (not that I'm talking about me).

Patience. It's a fantastic word when someone else talks about it, or when I am doling out advice like one doles out Halloween candy. But when it's applied to me, my face scrunches up a bit. I squirm in my yoga pants (yes, I wear yoga pants) when I am in the checkout line at the grocery store or waiting at a government office. I often think I am practicing patience, but I am really measuring out time in muted F-bombs.

When I got sober, I had to understand that there would be many situations where I simply would have no control over things. This is not an easy task for an egomaniac. I also had to learn to look at things from other people's points-of-views. Perhaps that slow, worn out cashier I was giving dagger eyes to had a sick child that was up all night. Maybe the meandering driver ahead of me on the road was lost and anxious. Perhaps the chatty neighbour was lonely and needed to talk to someone, and I happened to cross his path on the sidewalk. Taking that step back has helped me diffuse many a negative mindset. But I sometimes catch myself starting to get back into my egocentric, old thinking. "Is that cashier dumb? I am in a hurry!" "C'mon, stupid driver. Move!" "Oh, please get to the end of this story. I just want to get home to watch videos on YouTube."

All of those things involve *me*. I. Selfishness. And in the end, I get all bent out of shape for something that I can't control. My impatience slowly erodes and scruffs the edges of my serenity. My impatience puts me back in me—a frightening place to be for an alcoholic of my kind.

The word that attaches to this type of patience is "empathy." If I even try to understand where someone is coming from or perhaps their situation, I find it colours my own perception and places me in a gentler, kinder place. When I start to empathize a bit more, I find my impatience wanes.

There is also a deeper level of patience, that of interacting with others. If I can't control or change the lineup situation at Starbucks, I certainly can't control others and their own reactions and actions. I have tried that in the past, and it's like trying to push back the ocean with a feather duster. Trying to control all people and situations to suit me was a way of avoiding looking at myself. For this egomaniac, the idea of changing the whole world seemed a lot less daunting than changing myself. So when things didn't go "my way," my impatience level skyrocketed. I stomped away like a six-year-old with a three-year-old's maturity, wearing an infant's soiled diaper.

So knowing this, my patience with others takes on a different flavour. It's not like a lineup where I know that there is an end. Relationships are a bit more delicate than that, like playing Jenga on a life raft during hurricane season.

The word that attaches to this type of patience is "compassion." Compassion towards those in my life, whether I appreciate or even like them, brings me a new kind of patience. When I show this kind of patience to others who may or may not be in a good mental or emotional space, I am able to keep my own serenity and spiritual wellness intact. I don't engage at a level that takes me out of peace and understanding. I don't need to get into a Hulk Smash mode.

What it comes down to is expectations. When my expectations are trampled on (and they almost always are), I get impatient, irritable and annoyed, and then I go down the merry road of resentment. But before I hit that spot, I am edgy. I am short of fuse. I am testy. I get into the *-ISM* of my alcoholism: *I*. *S*elfish. *M*e. My patience is thin because my expectations are thick. When I expect one of my kids to be a perfect child, being peaceful and quiet, but instead they are having trouble with something or haven't had much sleep, my patience dissolves like tissue in a cup of chamomile. When I expect my wife to just let me do whatever I want and ignore what needs to be done, my patience is easily toppled. When I expect people to leave me alone in my office and just do their work without question, my patience slips away like a ninja in the night.

Dealing with my expectations really helps me with my patience. High expectations = low patience and high resentment. My ego may fight this, though. So, I carry spiritual principles into all of my affairs and I try to get right with myself. I want to be of service to others and to not fly off the mental handle. When I do show patience, through the lens of compassion, love and light, I am in a safer place, a gentler plane, a more serene landing spot.

When I finally delve one spot deeper on the patience depth chart, where I land is on the idea of being patient with myself and where I am in my new life.

The word that attaches to this type of patience is "self-love." As an active alcoholic, self-centred and selfish in my ways, I always wanted things *now*. Got it? Gimme now. Want it? Get it here. Don't have it? Take it right away. Alcohol was my way of getting instant and immediate relief from the torture of being me, to deal with the things around me that felt unapproachable in any other fashion. Those impulse buy carts at IKEA, with the 1000-pack tea lights and the left-handed parsley curlers, were made for people like me. Even when I didn't want it or need it, I wanted it and needed it right away. Alcohol satisfied my craving for something at that moment, when I wanted it, where I wanted it and how I wanted it, usually when I was alone and desperate. Self-loathing was my chaser. Alcohol was Desire's Holy Grail in liquid form, a quick fix measured out in shot glasses.

Wanting my life to be exactly how I want it now won't happen today. Wanting my dreams and wishes granted now won't happen today. This is where my deep patience lies. Knowing that I don't have all the answers now, knowing that

I can't foresee things, knowing that the direction of my life is out of my hands—these are the things I need to sit with and be okay with. And for the most part, I am. Certainly there are moments where I want to rush things. I want to know specific things. I want to know general things. I want, I want, I want. Patience, grasshopper. It all comes in His time, not mine. So sit, have a croissant and maybe a little espresso. Watch the clouds, contemplate the ground I stand on and feel the wind whistle past my ears. Practice self-love. Be kind to the man in the mirror.

And like my son with his LEGO, it's about breathing and just being with things, moment by moment. I see what is needed, do what is required at any time, and follow the directions from that voice in the back of my mind that tells me what is the right thing to do, no matter how much my ego protests. I build a life, block by block.

Patience.

Takeout for One

I once worked for a very prestigious and fancy restaurant. Ego ran rampant there, as one could imagine, and I was no different in that regard. I was on the upswing at that restaurant, and it was *management's* honour, not mine of course, that I worked for them at that hard-to-get-a-reservation establishment. The kitchen was a rough one to work in. No weak links need apply. The hours were tough, but manageable. The food was of high caliber, but that was not an issue for me. I was coming off of a great run at my last job and I had many accolades laid at my feet like rose petals. I felt unstoppable.

It wasn't long before I started to feel that very familiar out-of-place feeling wrap around me like a dirty rag. Where I was once the go-to guy, I felt like the get-lost dude. I didn't gel with anyone. No one laughed at my jokes. No one was impressed with my fine work and magnanimous nature. I pulled out all of my old parlour tricks: playing the social chameleon, lowering my standards, putting on a "brave" face, etc. I was surrounded by guys in starchy crisp whites, yet I felt alone.

I got into arguments. Plenty of them.

"You need to fire Jeff," I barked at my boss one day, as he passed by my station.

"Excuse me?"

"You need to fire Jeff. He's utterly useless. He can't cook worth shit. He slows me down during service. He's a walking disaster," I said as I prepped a foie gras terrine.

"That's a bit harsh, don't you think?" he asked, leaning on my work counter.

"No. He needs to go." I slammed my French knife down on the cutting board and stared down at the cleaned lobe of duck liver.

"Look, I get that you don't get along. But he drives 50 kilometers a day to get here and back. He can't afford to live in the city yet. He has a lot of passion."

"I don't give a *shit* about his passion. He can be a passionate crossing guard, then."

My boss turned away, scratched his arm, then looked back at me.

"Paul, just—"

"If you don't fire him, I am going to quit. It's either him or me."

The chef said nothing. He tried to smooth out the situation over the next few hours, but my mind had been made. I was caught up in the grandeur of me and of the resentment of them choosing that orange traffic cone of a cook rather than me, the Great I Am. I was wounded that they couldn't see the difference between a budding Chef Paul Bocuse and a hackneyed Chef Boyardee. My indignation simmered then boiled over. I tried to rally the troops to my cause, but found no takers. So I resigned myself to the fact that my genius was being neglected. I handed in my two weeks notice.

A couple of days before my last shift, I asked the guys if they wanted to grab a few drinks as a goodbye. I had drank with them before, so I knew that I was dialed into the right crowd—hard drinkers who didn't fear last call and who knew their way around adult beverages and how to get them after hours. They knew the sting of a Jägermeister but still stumbled into work the next day. They told me they would come.

I booked a table at the local Irish pub. As I headed out of the kitchen on that last shift, I reminded everyone to meet me there. They nodded as they continued to pump out the orders. They would be done soon, and we would toast the culinary stallion, me, who slipped through their grip. It would be a bittersweet end.

The pub was busy. It always was on Friday nights. I sat at the table of ten, alone. It was a still a bit early. People started to eye the table, setting their drinks on it. I pushed them away. I phoned my wife to come down to the pub. I wanted her to see just how missed I would be. I wanted her to revel in the glorious going away I would be having. I stared at my watch.

I called the kitchen from a pay phone. They said they were cleaning up and then they would be on their way. I hung up, clutched my Guinness and waited. My wife showed up. She ordered her drink and we sat there. I continued to glare at my watch, as if I were trying to teleport my co-workers through the airwaves. The drinks started to taste different as the night moved on. The hops in the beer were the same, but the bitterness seemed stronger. I wasn't tasting the beers as I was downing them to teleport myself to a holding cell where all noise ceased to bother me. My pride and ego took a beating while my anger flared up. No cold drink could put out those flames. I left the table to the onlookers—those who deserved it. I wouldn't need it.

For years this resentment clung to me like foam on the side of a Pilsner glass. I had problems reconciling who I thought I was to how I was treated. I couldn't see the connection between my perceived greatness and the piss-poor parade of wet confetti and limp noisemakers I had received. I held this moment like a faded Polaroid thumbtacked to a crumbled corkboard in my mind.

It wasn't until I started my journey of healing that I saw the real truth behind the situation. Clear and objective perception is a wonderful thing when dealing with a painful past, but it also acts as a cleaning agent; it removes the grime of wasted anger from the corners of the mind. It wipes away misdirected outrage and ego. It clears the path for more enlightened treading.

What was plain to see in this whole situation was my arrogance. I had made snap and harmful judgments of others. I had had a chip on my shoulder. I had played victim and, at the same time, I was grandiose. I had not been as professional as I had thought I was. I had taken things very personally. I had put people in awkward situations. I had belittled people publicly. I had unconsciously made sure that no one would show up at the pub to see me off, which fed into my woe-is-me story—the one which powered my life. No wonder no one wanted hang out with me. *I* wouldn't have wanted to hang out with me.

What I learned was that regardless of what parts others play in a situation, the only part I need to concern myself with is my mine and mine alone. I am in charge of taking responsibility for my shortcomings. I am in charge of how I can make amends, if necessary, and learn from my mistakes. I can only control my own reactions and future behaviour. It's a simple equation of taking care of the numbers in my column and nothing else. Don't carry the one. I have to let the One, the Creator, do the carrying and relieve myself of playing God.

Keeping resentment alive is a futile maneuver of misplaced energy and emotion. Holding on to the resentment of that day kept me down in the dirt for years. I played it out in my mind's eye and escalated their evil and my holiness. It was just another brick in the wall I had built around myself. Learning to let go of resentment and anger has been an exercise in wholesale emotional de-escalation and freedom. I no longer carry any hard feelings towards those ex-co-workers of mine, and that brings me much peace. I don't have to excuse them for their actions, but I have to just own my part of the ordeal and move on. And I have moved on. I don't wait in bars for people to carry me on their shoulders.

The take-away that night was powerful. Humble pie for one, please.

Street Sweeper

"If it falls your lot to be a street sweeper, sweep streets like Michelangelo painted pictures, sweep streets like Beethoven composed music, sweep streets like Leontyne Price sings before the Metropolitan Opera. Sweep streets like Shakespeare wrote poetry. Sweep streets so well that all the hosts of heaven and earth will have to pause and say: Here lived a great street sweeper who swept his job well. If you can't be a pine at the top of the hill, be a shrub in the valley. Be the best little shrub on the side of the hill."
~ **Martin Luther King Jr.**

When I was growing up and trying to figure out what I wanted to do with my life, I remember my parents telling me that no matter what I wanted to do or be, they would support me. If I wanted to be a piano player, they would buy me a piano and pay for lessons.

If I wanted to play hockey, they would drive me to rinks on cold Sunday mornings. But, they said that no matter what I chose to do I was to do it to the best of my ability. They said that if I wanted to be a garbage man ("sanitation worker" wasn't a term used back then), then I was to be the best garbage man I could be. Those words have always stuck with me.

As I moved through school, I felt the need to be the best at what I did. The drive to succeed wasn't based on ego or pride (although I did feel good about getting top marks in the class), but on the simple fact that I did what I loved and it came naturally to me. Studying, reading, memorizing—these were the tools of my innate curiosity about life. Whether it was dinosaurs, planets, electricity or any other science topic, my mind was pricked by the unknown and the desire to understand it. I found myself in gifted programs, science competitions and other geekfests, which I loved because I was surrounded by like-minded kids. There was no judgment.

I was crushed to find that I couldn't excel in everything I wanted to, like sports, arts or relationships. There was a disconnection or short circuit in my fuse box when it came to understanding that it was okay to not be first in everything. I couldn't relate to the idea of trying things for fun or continuing to do things for the joy of it rather than to get that first place medal. I did not understand how anyone could pursue anything unless they were aiming for the top dog position. My identity and self-esteem were wrapped up in where I stood in the pecking order, and I didn't like to get out of bed for anything less than top spot.

As an adult, I was blessed to be in a profession that I could pour my energy into and get rewarded for it. I sacrificed myself and important things in my life to ensure that I was the best employee wherever I worked. I stood out and I was pleased with that for a while. But, for someone with a soul-sickness like me, I needed to be treated extraordinarily just to feel ordinary. So I continued to drink even though I was achieving professional success. The disease of perception played tricks on me, and I felt that in some way I was still failing. I felt that I needed to do *more*. The ironic thing is that, in the end, the combination of my warped thinking and continued self-medicating brought upon me a deterioration of my skills, my reliability, my reputation and the trust others had in me. I was starting to become washed up.

At the same time, I found myself dipping my toes into new interests. When I found out that I couldn't master these interests the first time around, I gave up. I wasn't willing or interested to go through the early growing pains (and enjoyment) of learning new skills and toiling and getting into the muck of things. I was afraid of making mistakes and looking foolish. My fears tore at me like zombies on brains and halted any attempts to grow. Joy was as impossible to achieve unless alcohol was involved. And even then the party was starting to wane.

It wasn't until I started running, in my second year of recovery, that I understood the idea of doing something for the pleasure of it. I realized very early on that I wasn't going to win marathons or even get close to the times others ran, and that took the pressure off of me. I was focused on how I could better myself and enjoy the moving meditation that running provided me. I felt more in touch with the Creator and the spirit when I ran. I found that the holy triumvirate of body, mind and spirit was aligned when I ran. I didn't need to reach for anything other than my own potential.

This mindset brings me a more generous portion of humility to my plate. It opens up more venues to me. It allows me to see that the act of just doing is more important than recognition. Even when there are crowning achievements, they are fleeting. The shine wears off of them, whereas my deeper connection to myself and those around me is a lifelong buzz. I am no longer as attached to the accomplishments in my life as I am to the relationships I have forged with others, with my authentic self and with the Divine.

Like the street sweeper, I am where I need to be and who I need to be. I will probably never be rich or famous. While my ego bristles at that declaration, I have learned to be supplicant and to succumb to that notion. I have struggled in many ways with how many people I reach with my blog, podcast and all other quantifiable areas of my life. What I am learning is that it's not the quantity but the quality of people I can reach. When I near the end of my life, how will I measure myself? By how many numbers I could fit onto a spreadsheet or by the number of hearts I touched?

I recall doing a deep guided meditation and seeing my late Uncle Miguel in a garden. I asked him some questions, including "What is my purpose here on this Earth?" He put his hand on mine and said, "It's to make others feel good about themselves." And that was it. It wasn't to be a world class snowboarder or *New York Times* bestselling author, but to make others feel good about themselves. That's it. So that's the relay baton which has been passed to me. I have to run with it.

Today, I keep things in perspective. I remember that I am only here to be the best I can be. When I take my eyes off of that ideal and look at what others are doing, I get off-centre. I feel unbalanced. I just have to keep my side of the street clean. Sweep, sweep, sweep to the best of my ability.

Insecurity – Acceptance

"The curious paradox is that when I accept myself just as I am, then I can change."
~ **Carl Rogers**

"The reason we struggle with insecurity is because we compare our behind-the-scenes with everyone else's highlight reel."
~ **Steve Furtick**

Dodging and Burning

I have always loved photography. I cut my teeth back in the days before Photoshop became required for anyone working a lens. I played with chemicals and darkrooms and spent countless hours developing paper in washes and acids, which was both exciting and painfully tedious. There were no "erase" buttons on the cameras back then. I just hoped that the f-stops and depth-of-field calculations were correct. I'd bracket shots to hedge my bets. Having plenty of film on hand and relying on judgment and training were the bare minimum requirements to capture a semi-decent picture.

The one thing anyone needs to know about photography is that it's all about light. That's it. If we control the intensity and amount of light then we can snap a full range of photos, from the mundane to the profound and the dingy and dirty to the sharp and pristine. We adjust, tweak and flat out make a mess of errors to see things the way that we think we see them or want to see them.

We have many filters.

Reflection, refraction, refocus.

Two men came into my life a few years ago, at roughly the same time.

As I look into the lens of the time that has spanned since, I can see two different series of snapshots developing slowly before me, each with a variety of hues and shadows. I await to see what turns to dark tones and what careens towards light and brightness. Most photos are balanced, but some are not.

Snapshot #1: I meet with Don. It is clearly his first meeting, and I sit one seat from him. We speak during and after the meeting. I urge him to pick up a 24-hour chip, which is given to newcomers. I give him my phone number and we part ways, imbued with the energy one has when they have spoken to someone new to recovery, charged with the ions that float through a spirit that feels that they have perhaps touched another in a small way. Moonlight shines brightly.

Snapshot #2: I meet Elijah through my old treatment centre. We speak several times on the phone about recovery, life, children, wives and booze. He likes to talk, a lot. The Creator has dropped a time bomb of patience and listening development right into my waiting lap. Elijah and I plan to meet at the one-year medallions of one of my sponsees. I am filled with the warmth that courses through one when they have found a kindred comrade of sorts. Dusk's cool light bounces off storefronts. Faint halos surround buildings.

Two darkroom techniques I learned in college were burning and dodging. When the light doesn't hit the film the way I want, I can manually etch more light onto the film (a.k.a. burning) or I can block out the light (a.k.a. dodging). These techniques allow me to control, adjust and balance light on the finished product. I also played with pushing and pulling film to deliberately under- or over-expose the film and then under- or over-developing the film. This is for effect in playing with texture and contrast.

The idea behind these ways of manipulating light, shade and exposure is to correct what we see as flaws in the pictures. We get to put Humpty Dumpty back together again, if need be, by horsing around with these methods. Control, control and control until the photo gets to be the way we imagined it in the first place.

Snapshot #1A: I text and call Don once or twice. I ask him to do some reading before we meet next time. He agrees to meet at a coffee shop a few days later, where we chat for a while on a bench. He hasn't read anything yet, but I share my experiences, my lows, my highs, my recovery work and my ways of keeping sober. He has few questions. He is conciliatory and agreeable. He admits that he is unsure if he should go to the cottage for the weekend because drinks will be served there. I advise him to stay away from booze for a while. Silence. Branches sway in the breeze. A car zooms by. The light is dimming over the clouds. It might rain. Fuzzy lines on the horizon.

Snapshot #2A: Elijah calls me daily and leaves me messages. He wants to meet up. "How does this thing work, this recovery?" he asks. We speak several times over a few days. He is anxious, excited and frightened at the same time. He's my kind of guy. He hits up meetings and joins a group. He is starting to get excited about life again. Static hits the line on our last call. A solar flare, perhaps. A burst of light zapping our conversation. Burning bright blasts hit the screen.

The darkroom was the perfect place for me because I had a reason to be alone, to be isolated and to be in connection with something that I could finally control and overcome. I could sense a mastery of self and other things. I could doctor and shape forms. I was in control of what lay at my fingertips, and through association I unconsciously felt that I could control the forms and thoughts in my mind. I could stop the chattering, dodge the realities and fears, burn through the cravings and desires, push my limits and ego and pull back from engagements and life itself. I was exposed in the wrong light. I didn't know who I was or what I was. Drinking helped me try to figure it out. Drinking was the liquid I dropped my blank self into and I hoped to see the shape of a human come out.

Snapshot #1B: I convince Don to meet me at the local coffee shop. He brings his 14-month-old child. We try to do some work from the recovery text. It is near impossible to work with his daughter demanding attention. I ask him to mark up his book with his pencil, but he doesn't. He tells me that he drank on the weekend at the cottage. We talk about it. I then tell him that I will take him to a meeting later that night and that I will give him an old stroller of my children's for his child. He later tells me that he is going to bed early. I drop off the stroller regardless. I smell beer on his breath. Shadows lurk in the corners. Lines are fading. Exposure is spotty. The lens is clouded.

Snapshot #2B: I meet Elijah at a deli to talk about recovery. I can barely get a word in edgewise; he is hopped up on fear, excitement and nervousness. He is unbridled in his seeking. He descends upon me with countless questions. He wants it all and he wants it now. He is a sponge in search of a sea. He wants to do the work immediately. I ask him to read some pages. He jots them down then jumps out of his seat to meet his friends. I ride my bike in the light of a fading crescent. Features are highlighted. Light is focused at the rims of the darkness.

In the end, these snapshots and these two men developed the way they were meant to develop. Unlike the pictures I took in college, these kinds of projects are not in my realm of manipulation. I don't get to shape and control them. I don't have the power to have them seize sobriety or not. I don't have the equipment, will or tools to convert black and white into colour.

I am not the principal photographer for those snapshots or those men. I am just a reflection of His light. I can't control the photos in my own photoshoot of recovery, either, but I can adjust the lighting. In working with others, I can open things up or I can squeeze the aperture closed with selfishness, unwillingness or ego. My life is an ever-developing roll of film. A few bad frames don't define my life.

Willingness and unwillingness—they define how much light I allow into my life. Willingness allows me to go as far as I need to go to maintain my recovery. Willingness is the basic tenet to becoming well. I pray for all of the people in my path. I pray for willingness in us all, to push towards a higher exposure. We can never have enough willingness, the will to want it all. Willing to want it all depends on what we bring to the ocean of recovery: a thimble or a bucket.

Today, another string of photos pass me by. What light do I shed upon it or allow others to shed on it? What's my focus? Where's the lens pointed?

The Fire Inside

"Sexual Misconduct." The words popped out at me as I read the email.

The school sent all the parents a note regarding the arrest of a young man who worked at the school as a lunch supervisor. He had allegedly sexually interfered with a six-year-old boy while babysitting him.

I visited the police website and it was mentioned that the man worked exclusively with children. The police believed there were more victims. They showed his picture. He was a child himself, with scraggly facial hair resembling a worn bristle pad. His eyes were a distant blue. Medium-length, red hair partially covered his flushed cheeks.

He didn't look like what most imagine when they think of a

sexual predator. *Alleged* sexual predator.

Then again, what *does* a predator look like?

I looked into this kid's face, into his eyes. I tried to find the humanity in that mug shot. I searched the picture as if to coax out his pain, to source why he had done the things he had done. This is something I do all the time, whether it's a petty thief or a serial killer. I try to find that little nugget of compassion for them, something that I can try to grow into something meaningful.

It's not easy. Sometimes I wonder what the point of that spiritual exercise is. Maybe I am trying to relate too much. Maybe I hope that the person will have a second shot at life. Maybe I just want reassurance that we're not all a bunch of Neanderthals, clubbing one another into oblivion. I know that people make bad decisions. There is a scale, of course, that "bad decisions" are stretched upon. Having a third slice of cake can be seen as a poor choice, but molesting a child? Stabbing someone? We're talking about the other end of the spectrum's behaviours.

It's a stretch.

There are many people who would easily throw the match to the pyre in a public square and think nothing of it. Let the bastards burn, they'd say. But I have a soft spot for those who are maladjusted to living. I made many bad decisions in my active drinking days. I made questionable choices and had many unacceptable behaviours, including criminal behaviours. Was I a bad man? Should I be heaped onto the pile of wood, flesh and flame?

I too have a mug shot.

It's perception. If my child is molested, all of my spiritual nature may go out the window. Folks may have to stop me from using a shovel to beat that molester to near death. Who's to say that people didn't want to do the same when I drove drunk with my own three-and-a-half-year-old in the car? Is it pointless to try to find that glow of good in others? I know it exists, even in the most evil of people. It may be a dying ember, but it's there. It gives me hope, even in the face of tragedy.

People ask why bad things happen to good people. Where is God when children are being hurt or when people are victimized by horrid crimes? He doesn't act because of free will. We were given free will. People act according to their ego, pride, rage, and the myriad of other things that fall under their free will. My understanding is that God is involved in the healing, not the crimes. God is there when people help others. God is there when we rise above our pain and help others. God is there when we rise above the dirt.

I like to think that God was there when people reached out to me and helped me in my darkest days, even with the weight of my history and actions resting heavily on my shoulders. People still saw that light of good in me.

That is why I always seek the same in others. I know it's there. Of course, some folks need to be permanently taken away from the rest of society. Some people are beyond help or rehabilitation. But that doesn't mean there isn't that little spark inside, underneath all of the pain, anger and misery.

What I find is that it's in my best emotional and spiritual interest to see the flame of good in everyone. It doesn't absolve people of their misdeeds, but it gives me pause to reflect on our humanity, our frailty and our weakness. In the face of these things, I see the resiliency, the faith and the merciless kindness in others. This is what lights my spirit. This is the human condition in its entirety.

Somewhere in those mug shot eyes, there is a flame.

I know there is.

What the General Said

"If you choose not to decide, you still have made a choice."
~ **Rush, "Freewill"**

The simplest and easiest way to make me have a fainting spell was to ask me to make a decision. To ask me anything beyond what pair of shoes I planned on wearing that day (it was always running shoes, by the way) would put me into a tailspin. Decision-making was meant for those who had confidence, the type that could crush cars like Thor. I wasn't a decision maker. I was a decision avoider.

I used to work at a large and prestigious hotel in the city, and would marvel at how my fellow managers could make big and bold decisions. I was easily impressed, and annoyed, by the moxie that some of these managers had to stampede ahead with poor information, limited vision and giant *cojones* large enough to swing over their shoulders liked a gym bag. I didn't understand the idea of making decisions with less than a full and complete grasp of the situation, perhaps combined with a summit meeting, a dump truck full of well-researched reports and some divine guidance. Even with all of that, the idea of making and following through with a decision would still bring on a flurry of fears. Big fears.

A few years ago, I read a short primer on leadership[1] by former United States secretary of state and general, Colin Powell. He spoke of the 40-70 rule: Have no less than forty per cent of the information you need to make a tough decision and no more than seventy per cent. If you have less than forty per cent, you are highly likely to make a mistake. If you wait to have more than seventy per cent, the opportunity may pass and someone else may beat you to the punch. The idea is that our intuition will carry us through that other thirty per cent. General Powell also mentioned that leaders *will* make mistakes, but the goal is to have more right decisions than wrong ones.

I balked at the idea of going with my gut on less than one

---

[1] General Colin Powell, A Leadership Primer. Retrieved from http://www.think-energy.net/Colin-Powell-on-Leadership.pdf

hundred per cent of the information. I didn't trust my instinct any more than I did the guy at the subway station who tries to scam beer money off of me by recounting his I-just-got-out-of-prison-and-have-no-money-to-get-home sob story. I didn't trust myself because I had no sense of self-worth. Who would trust a booze-pig? If my own intuition was driving me into dark passages, then how could I make sound business decisions and lead my team in the charge?

One of my greatest fears was the fear of looking stupid. But when I unfolded this fear I could see that what I feared more was looking like an imposter. I feared that someone was going to rip my mask off and reveal to the world the joke that I felt I was. I was a body snatcher, an alien playing an adult, playing me. I felt like a set of Russian dolls—every layer was just candy coating around the tiny, insignificant, true me. The rest was glitter and paint.

The fear of being a fraud haunted me. I didn't know who I was, so I certainly couldn't trust the face I glued on in the morning. I needed alcohol to numb myself before facing the world. I needed to quell the feeling of spiritual scarcity and the darkness in my soul. Although I did well in my profession, I felt a great sense of inadequacy. I attributed any success in my professional or personal life to blind luck. I put down anyone who tried to compliment me. I downplayed any successes I had, minimizing my contribution. I shrank as small as I possibly could, so to do what The General said would have been to make a lemming's leap into the abyss. It went against everything I felt about myself.

I often made bold and brazen decisions about *not* making decisions. It kept me in a holding pattern, it kept me from stepping on any toes and it kept me from facing my fears. What it also did was backfire. When I was unwilling to make decisions, no one knew where they stood with me. I was a walking vague question mark. I was often told I was a nice guy but not a good leader. I wasn't worthy of being a foot soldier in The General's army.

On my journey of recovery and reclaiming my spirit, I have begun to see that The General was right. As I learn to stand in my own space, I see that the need to be absolutely right to the point of paralysis is a way of sabotaging my growth. I need to see past my ego and embrace the fact that not only can I be wrong, but I can also be right. I see that my intuition is a great conduit for my authentic self. By making firm decisions, big and small, I start to find my own voice. I start to see that others are willing to follow, because they pick up on my growing self-assurance. I have learned the difference between cockiness and confidence. I am starting to feel for myself what it is that others have always seen in me, nudging closer and closer to my higher self, the self that I was created to be.

The real imposter for all of these years was the façade my ego imposed on me. I saw myself as a certain way and allowed myself to be swayed by that false ideal. Now, the more I allow myself to make mistakes, to build trust in myself and to have others hold trust in me, the more I push myself to prosper while humbly accepting my imperfections, and the less I feel like an imposter. I feel more complete, more intact and more like *me*.

While I don't have the exact percentages of my wholeness to back my progress up, I am sure that The General would be happy to hear that I've been moving forward in the trenches, losing a few battles here and then but still winning the war.

Onward soldier.

Man Up, Buttercup

I've always had a tenuous relationship with the idea of manhood. Or at least with the theory of manhood and all that it entails to be "a man." I think it's difficult for some of us dudes to understand what is expected of us at the best of times, but it is doubly difficult when you're a confused and drunk man, like I was. Hell, I had a hard time being a human being, let alone fitting into a gender role defined by no one and everyone. Or, maybe gender had nothing to do with it. Maybe I was just a jerk.

Growing up, I didn't have a large family. My father worked a lot of shift work and we didn't see him much. As a teenager, I was out when he was home. But, my father was, and still is, a loving man who provided for his family and did the best he could with two boys in a country that he wasn't raised in, speaking its language.

I wasn't surrounded by many adult males. Most of my teachers were females. The men in the neighbourhood worked and the women stayed at home. In many ways, that suited me fine; I enjoyed the gentle yet forceful female energy. Being a shy kid, I was able to nestle in that and feel safe.

I went to an all-boys Catholic school and found harsh and immediate rejection as the smart, weirdly-dressed kid. Bullying wasn't seen the way it is today, so my pleas for help fell on mostly deaf ears. The general advice given was to get over it. "Stop being a sissy, boy. Grow a pair." The teachers who were looked up to at my school were jocks, and the ones who were often ridiculed were more sensitive and creative. I felt that I had little chance in finding refuge.

I didn't realize it at the time, but I was starting to feel that there was something lacking in my life. I had started drinking in high school, but it wasn't with any kind of regularity. I drank heavily when I bothered to get drinks, but I could also go for a while without wanting. It was the only time in my life where alcohol was a take-it-or-leave-it proposition. That changed soon after graduation.

My luck with the girls was on par with my abysmal attempt at befriending guys. When it came to women, I didn't know what to say or what to do. I didn't even bother. I knew my chance of getting a date was the same as catching typhoid fever. Alcohol did not need any wooing or courting; it was just there, always available, its dance card always empty and ready for me to stamp it.

I didn't drink because I was without brotherhood or the company of women. This failed sense of manhood didn't get me drunk any more than the colour of my car did. It was just a part of a greater whole for me. Being a man was something I didn't know anything about. I felt sexless, like a eunuch. There was no instruction manual for this kind of thing.

The idea of manhood plagued me into my adulthood. Being a husband, son and father didn't magically imbue me with the mysterious formula of being a man. I didn't see myself as fully capable of anything, subservient to everyone, and I walked around as the shell of a man I thought I deserved to be. I couldn't be with women and I couldn't relate to men. I saw men on TV shows and in movies being mocked, seen as dumb, needy man-children who needed to have the firm, solid, and level-headed touch of a woman to make them whole. I eventually started to resent both men and women for the power that I put on them. I hated myself for being the weak, pathetic excuse for a man I had become. Worthless.

You can imagine my disdain whenever someone told me to "man up." I would have manned up if only I'd known how to.

It wasn't an IKEA bookshelf with some diagrams and an Allen key. At the same time, I found the expression repugnant and offensive. To "man up" meant that I was currently anything but a man, that I was being sensitive, empathetic, creative and other things not seen as masculine. To "man up" meant playing into the stereotype of a hard-ass dude—unflinching, emotionally unavailable and only interested in anything that is dripping with testosterone. Anything less than that twisted idea of manhood equated failure. I found myself resenting the phrase itself and what it expressed.

I felt like there were two realities: the unreachable masculinity that infected society and the wonky one I lived in, where I cried at dog food commercials and ate ladyfinger biscuits while sewing buttons back on cushions. There was a great fault line between the two. I often fell in there, which I felt was of my own making. Deep down, I did know that something wasn't right and that putting an unrealistic pressure on myself was downright cruel.

I don't know exactly when things started to turn in my recovery, but they just did. That sense of shame and of being less than all started to go away. I was working with others, reading, praying, meditating and repairing relationships. The biggest relationship to repair was, and continues to be, the one with myself.

I started to see that being a man wasn't what externals dictated or what was observed on the big screen or in popular culture. It wasn't the collective portrait and resume of what a man should or should not be. It was just to be me—to be a solid, present and loving person who happens to be male. It is to treat myself, fellow men and, more importantly, women with respect, understanding and compassion. I don't feel the separation of us and them anymore. I don't feel the separation of myth and reality anymore.

I have learned how to be a loving male in the fellowship of spirituality and recovery. The men in recovery groups showed me through actions how to treat them and others. They showed me that we can say "I love you" to one another, hug one another and shoulder another man's head while he cries. There is no shame in these actions. It's not how much we bench press that makes us men, but how much empathy and love we can carry on our backs. It's not the hairs on our face that measure our manliness, but how we face our fears.

These are the things that I want to show my own two boys. These are what I hope they will see. I pray that they will see the wholeness of life not through the filters of gender but through the power of trust in oneself.

Clamming Up

When I was in my teens and early 20s, I hung out with a few people who I reluctantly called friends. They were primarily drinking buddies, but since we had gone to high school together we let that thin thread of history bind us as friends. When we weren't hitting it hard at the bar or hitting on the ladies, we were hitting the books (we succeeded at the first, failed miserably at the second and survived the third). We were together because no one else would have us.

We were the school's lowest caste, the untouchables, the diseased drifters of the hallways without a whiff of cool factor to anchor us socially. We were misfits who shared misery with a pint of ale and a cup of moaning. Although our Gang of Losers badge kept us connected, there was also an unwritten code that pervaded our little Shire and kept us sick. It was a silent code, but it was absolutely saturated with quiet rage. It was a virus that was always active in our collective psyche and ready to strike with viciousness that left its victims paralyzed. It was deadly stuff.

Growing up, I had always been good at school. I loved the smell of textbooks, the creasing of new notepad paper and the chalk dust that I stepped on when writing an answer on the board. I enjoyed writing essays, taking tests and studying. These spoke to me at a deeper level than just trying to look good or get attention. I didn't like too much attention, so I was rather quiet about my above average marks. When I moved to a new school in Grade 7, things changed dramatically. The kids at my new school didn't appreciate the new smart kid who entered their midst. The kids were almost twice my size and their hobbies included cars, classic rock and kicking the shit out of one another. Anything outside of that holy trinity of testosterone was seen with equal parts confusion and disdain. I saw all fists and no handshakes that year.

But, there was something I learned there. A big lesson.

I was good at equations and did well at adding things up. I learned a very important equation that year in school. It was possibly the only thing I was able to retain that year, and it didn't come from a textbook:

Being yourself = pain.

Simple yet profound.

Math hurt.

So, it was in my best interest to go underground, to shield myself and to turtle and live in a den safe from the predators. I was, for the first time, wounded deeply. When I tried to address it to adults, it got worse. So I hid. I kept replaying the new equation in my head, just in case I dared venture into trying something new or open my beaten down shell to let someone in. You could keep knocking, but you weren't getting in. Ever.

Years later, when I was hanging out with my "friends," we had a dangerous game that asked, "Who can get the worst dirt on someone else in the group?" You could not make mistakes, open up or show any kind of vulnerability at all. We held each other up to those same equations. If one of us messed up in any fashion at all, big or small, and it was witnessed by any one of us, then that transgression was immediately banked and used against the person for life. We never let up or let you forget what you did. If anything, we turned the tourniquet even tighter if the person bemoaned being reminded about whatever happened. There was no need to have resentments because there was always someone there to recite your painful and embarrassing moments to you all day and night. It was a sick circle of shame and abuse.

If I showed a tear, if I was upset or if I verbalized that I was lonely, it was instant torture fodder for the fellas. We stunted each other's growth with inhuman welts caused by the verbal cat-o-nine-tails tethered to us at all times. We couldn't show each other the slightest tinge of humanity, lest it be beat out of us. And these were my *friends*. These were the people whom I felt safest with in my life. But, I was no victim. I was just as ruthless, if not the most vengeful of the pack. My way with words ensured that I could flail you with flowery prose and let you still feel the thorns. If I could make you cry, even better.

Deep down, I pined for the relationships the other people around me had, ones that were supportive, enjoyable, relaxing and brotherly. The only time I felt arms around me was when someone was giving me a WrestleMania-like takedown on the concrete during recess. So, I learned that being tough and being a little shit took away the threat of getting hurt. Stay clammed up or get shut up the hard way.

My drinking escalated and I soon realized that I didn't need those guys any more. I didn't need them to beat me up and tell me what a rotten deal I was for being human, because I could do that on my own. I was better at it than they ever could be. I became the jailer, inmate, warden and in-house torturer. The executioner came to play every day.

Coming into my recovery and spiritual path, one of the things I have learned is that I am meant to be the way I was created. There was never anything wrong with me, even if everything pointed to that conclusion. I still have a lot of work to do to get to my true core. But with the Creator now in my life and running the show, I can do what I need to do to help myself and, more importantly, to help others. I have learned to show and express the little boy who just wanted to be who he was meant to be, who wanted to play and to be seen. I have learned new equations and have met some wonderful new teachers, guides and mentors in my life. I am back in school in so many ways.

I am careful of who I let in my life. The people I call friends truly are friends. They support and encourage me. They nourish me. They are the light of God and faith. They work for the Creator, doing for me what I cannot do for myself, something I thought alcohol could do. There are no façades or walls to put up against my friends. There is no need to pretend to be someone else. I can cry, show my vulnerability and unwrap the wounds to show them the shrapnel. They soothe me and they complete me, and they show me the ways in which they have healed. In return, I do the best I can to reciprocate what they give me. I still struggle with this, as I am apt to hide away. I am still working through the old wounds, the old ways. I still clutch onto my hermetic ways. I still feel like people only want to be close to me so that their punches are swifter and closer to the chest. I know in my heart that this is not the case, but moving through fear and into faith is one of my challenges on this new path.

I no longer feel the need to clam up, even if my shell does close up around me at times. The light of joy and friendship is too bright to want to shut it out.

Isolation – Service

"*Solitude is feasting on God. Isolation is feasting on yourself.*"
~ **Stuart Greaves**

"*Service is the rent we pay for being. It is the very purpose of life, and not something you do in your spare time.*"
~ **Marian Wright Edelman**

The Bubble

If there is one thing, and one thing alone, that would make me think twice about picking up again, it would be the Bubble. Like most good alcoholics worth their tequila salt, I didn't "scare straight." They used to have TV shows where they paraded troubled teens through menacing prisons, with inmates who looked like Mr. T, roared like Hulk Hogan and were built like the Rock (and that was just the women). They gave the kids a quick taste of what prison life was like with the idea of frightening them into getting their act together. They got into the kids' faces, screamed at them and told them what happens to pretty little things like them inside prison walls.

Did it work? I am not sure. I know that if there was an equivalent for drinking, then it would have failed to shock me into sobriety. I performed my own version of trying to scare myself sober; I often looked online to see what the damage alcohol did to the body. I watched gory images of destroyed livers, of mangled car wrecks and of people literally dying of alcoholism. On the TV show *Intervention,* I watched as families pleaded and begged their loves ones to stop drinking. I could see the harm and destruction alcoholism caused, and yet I still drank while staring at the screen. I couldn't make the connection between me and those other people. *I was different.*

I drank after every painful and unsettling landmark in my life: after getting arrested, losing my family, visiting the hospital, having work issues, making and breaking promises to loved ones, having health issues…bottom after bottom after bottom. I clearly still needed more pain. Anyone in their right mind would have stopped much sooner. I was not in my right mind and hadn't been so in a very long time. So, when I had my last drink session—a pathetic, lonely, sad and unremarkable drinking session—I finally agreed to go to detox. I just couldn't take the pain any more.

* * *

I was driven to the hospital and handed over to a nurse for my intake. They examined my belongings with an eye that Hercules Poirot would have been envious of, and they filled out binders of paperwork. I had everything taken away except for my pajamas and slippers. My dignity had been stripped off long ago. I was placed in a room with ten beds, a washroom and a small table filled with paltry carbohydrate and sugar-laden snacks. That was it. It was as sparse as it was depressing. What made the room remarkable was the huge glass wall that separated us sickos from the fastidious and silent medical marshals who watched our every move, who monitored our actions and reactions and who doled out the medication on schedule. We were the watched. Every part of me wanted to leave right away, to get back in the car with my parents and to have them take me home to eat plain pasta and to cry myself to sleep. I also knew that I needed to be in the Bubble. It was the closest to a true scared straight moment I'd ever had.

The next few days were the worst I had ever felt. I had been used to hangovers and withdrawal symptoms, but detoxing was something special. Alongside the usual running cold and, the hot sweats, the heart palpitations, the dry mouth, the shakiness and the stomach aches, I had a charming case of the DT's (delerium tremens). I heard what I thought was a hockey game going on in the next room. I could clearly hear the chanting and cheers of the crowd. I could hear the announcer (Bob Cole, to be exact) calling the action. On the walls and ceiling, I saw blue worms. They squirmed with every breath I took.

I tossed and turned in my bed, desperate for sleep. It did not come. My mind was too sprung on excitatory neurotransmitters and barrels full of fear. Insomnia gripped me like it never had in my life. I watched in envy as the addicts seemed to sleep forever, rarely stirring. My mind and heart felt like they were being put through a blender and then into an extruder.

I read a lot. I don't remember what I read, but I know that after four entire days and nights of being up I had finished three novels.

I ate dry tuna salad sandwiches.

I popped blue pills and drank room temperature water. I watched other men come and go. I saw one man spend 45 minutes doing intake then walk in, look around and walk right back out. I was envious of his bold decision. I hid in the washroom when the creepy guy in the bed across from me frantically masturbated, which seemed to happen whenever he woke up.

I talked myself out of several withdrawal-induced panic attacks. I stared at the watchers watching me. I gazed into my own soul and found something wanting. I found an empty shell where a human used to reside.

I tried to eat chips.

Many times I attempted to leave the isolation and get into

"general population." I begged, I whined and I got indignant. Nothing worked. They just asked me to extend my arms out, and when my hands continued to violently tremble they gave me a pill and said they would check in on me later.

I prayed the whole time, shaky hands clenched in an even shakier attempt at supplication. I alternated between praying to die and praying that this was just a nightmare that I would wake up from. The pain—physical, mental, emotional and spiritual—was unbearable. I didn't know how to be. I didn't know who I was, what time it was or what day it was. I was truly lost. My compass, like my soul and heart, was broken. I could feel every molecule in me squeezed out, tensed up and bleeding out, broken. I invited death, yet fought to move away from it at all costs.

I ate more chips.

I knew that this was the last stop on the booze car train. I had gone through withdrawals before. I had gone through the cycles of guilt, shame and remorse, and I had experienced a lot of emotional pain before. This was different. It was the first time I could feel myself cry out for more than just a handout, a temporary fix or a shot in the arm to just move on. It was the first time I felt true desperation. It was the first time in my life that I felt utterly and completely hopeless. It was in the Bubble that I confessed to my innermost self that I was done with alcohol for good. Done.

I had finally turned some cosmic corner in my life. It was the last domino to fall. It was plugging in the last piece of the jigsaw puzzle together and finally seeing the entire picture. In that darkness, I was able to see a tiny pinpoint of hope and light. I had no choice in the matter. It was look towards that hope or die an alcoholic death. I felt the Creator near me for the first time, and I didn't know it at the time, but I knew I needed not be tethered to self-will any more. Something better was planned for me.

The ironic thing about the Bubble is that while I was physically trapped and peered at by others, by the end of it I felt a sense of freedom. I felt a sense of healing. I felt a sense that even though my conditions were dire and I had a lot of work to do on the outside, my inner life was going to have a explosive shift. I also felt that I was now being guided. A sense of ease came over me even before I was able to walk out of the room and join the others who were finishing detox. I was both frightened and calm.

The Bubble may be a place I never want to visit again, but what I got from it was more than I ever bargained for. And for that, the Bubble will always be a part of me. Except this time, I am on the outside, peering in through the lens of love and compassion and knowing that I have been kept around for a reason.

Every alcoholic I meet and help in any way is my reason.

I am free of the Bubble.

I Don't Need You

I *don't need you.*

This was my mantra—my warrior code. This was the mortar in my wall that I used to block you out. I didn't need you. I never did before, so why would I now? I liked to be the macho guy, the martyr who suffered (oh, did I suffer), so that you could see that I was strong. I resented getting assistance of any kind; I would have rolled around on hot nails rather than ask for help. Help was for the weak. Every man for themselves. Yet, deep down, I felt weak, pathetic and like less of a man. I was worthless, yet I thought I could still save myself. I wanted to show everyone that I was made of sandpaper. I was the anchor of the S.S Lone Wolf. Still I felt that I couldn't do right by me or anyone else. Failure followed me at every turn.

I drank.

Leave me alone.

This was the coat I wore, the mask I painted on and the kryptonite I poured into my veins to keep you at bay and away from me. My eyes, deadened already from pain and drink, seared into others the need for me to be left the hell alone. If that wasn't successful, my words would impale and deflect like a Viking in battle. I was afraid that if you got to know me in any way, you would run from me. So, I sent you packing before you could hurt me. I won. But I was the only one playing the game. I only defeated myself. I isolated myself to seal the deal.

I drank.

I don't need help.

I was a legend in my own mind and didn't need anyone to come in and play the stud when the lead role was already mine. Hit the bricks, pal. I had full control over everything, including my drinking. Oh, sure, there were some rough patches, and who doesn't have a bad day now and then? We go through phases, don't we? Even the hero gets sissy-slapped around now and then—one can't always carry the championship belt. It was nothing that a few drinks couldn't fix, or a few drinks more. I didn't need anyone to tell me what the deal was with anything in my life, because I had it all figured out. I just needed time to figure it out. I just needed some space to unlock the truth, to crack open my own true self and to hot-wire my heart to beat a little stronger.

I drank.

I need help.

Please help me…I'm dying…and I don't want to die like this.

Where did it all go wrong? The pain, the suffering, the hurt, and the lashes and gashes at my soul and spirit buckled my knees. Fears flapped around me like gulls on the pier, and the ideas of living with the drink or living without the drink had brought me to the point of insanity. I was crazed and defeated. I felt like I was dying. My alcoholism was suicide-by-inches. It was a matter of time. I couldn't do it anymore. I was done.

I couldn't drink.

I want to help you.

Is that really me thinking this?

If there is something that I have learned during my time in recovery is that I need to work with others. I need to help other people. I need to carry the message of hope. I need to use my past hurts and healings to help someone else turn their hurts to healings. I am only an ex-drunk, someone whose light-from-dark tale can perhaps illuminate someone else's dwelling of pain and sorrow.

Many men and women have done things for me that I can never pay back. They have spent countless time, energy and/or money trying to help me, or they stood right by me and watched as I burned my life to the ground yet one more time. But, they never left. There are so many who have hung around, who have picked me up when I wanted anything else but that and who actually gave a damn about me when I couldn't even look at myself in the mirror. There aren't enough dollars or days in me to pay back what has been bestowed upon me from those who have and still want to help me.

How can I help you?

What I can do is pay it forward. I can give to the next person who needs a jump-start. I can give to the next person who feels that they're alone. I can give to the next person who just requires someone to tell them that things do indeed get better. It's my mandate, my payment for being on this earth and my need to give someone else the idea that we humans are good at heart. By helping others I am healing my own wounds. By being of assistance to others in need I can see them in me and me in them, and I feel that connection. We aren't surrounded by glass, but we can see our reflection in others.

I need to help you.

When I help someone else, especially an alcoholic, I get out of myself, plain and simple. I am not spinning, thinking of myself and or ingesting copious amounts of Vitamin "I." I am being useful—something I never was before. I contribute. I show love and compassion rather than bare my teeth and growl when asked to be near someone and take in their humanness. I can be of service to someone who was once like me. If you're like me—refusing help, not needing anyone and not feeling deserving of love and attention—that's alright. I will still be here with arms waiting to close tightly around you as I whisper to you, "You are needed."

I need you.

Lone Wolf

When my oldest son was a toddler, he loved his bedtime tales. We read him simple, repetitive and short books. While we tired of them quickly, he was endlessly fascinated by the zesty words, the radiant pictures and the playful inflections in our voices as we tried to razzle dazzle him with these little stories. He asked for the same ones, over and over again. We obliged.

As he got older, the stories changed. They got more involved, the pictures were in more detail and the tales grew to be more complex. "A for Ant" soon turned into Curious George chasing bunnies, which turned into dinosaurs attacking other dinosaurs. Rawr.

Just like my son, I know that there are stories that I have told myself over and over again. Except that they weren't always at bedtime. But bedtime was certainly when they flourished most, because it was easier to let the tape play out in full technicolour majesty, complete with Gore-Tastic Smell-O-Vision. There's nothing like lying in the dark, letting the bogeyman from within rip me apart, again and again

We all have these stories, of course, consisting of the lies we tell ourselves, the fantastic creations that we buy into and the garbage that we polish over and over again (which still remains rubbish). "I'm not good enough," "I'm never going to amount to anything," "They're all after me," etc. The usual self-sabotaging beat down that we bring down on ourselves. Half of my brain manufactures bullshit and the other half buys it. Supply and demand. I was a grand wizard at that stuff. I found it was easy to punctuate all of those stories by getting hammered and showing the world what a piece of shit I was.

Self-fulfilling prophecy, n'est-ce-pas?

One of the stories I always told myself was that I didn't need anyone else and that I was fine on my own. I was a steely and wily wolf, a Charles Bronson-esque archetype, a Duke of Badass-ery. This worked perfectly in my favour as an active alcoholic, prolific introvert and avoider of social situations. I got to play that role that ill-suited me, and I suffered for it. I couldn't pull off the trick, and I found myself miserable and unable to survive much on my own, although I found being alone was my default setting.

There was no darker spot for me to be in than when I both craved community and yet feared it like a crate of snakes. That was the great friction in my life; I so wanted to be with others, but they frightened me. The tall tale I told myself was that I didn't need them: look at how great my life was without those people getting things messy with their needs, their weaknesses, their wanting or their drama. It was a clean sheet without emotions or expectations getting in the way. Also, I had more free time to drink.

But, wait. Was I not just projecting myself onto others? The neediness, the weaknesses, the wanting and the drama? That was me—my baggage. Perhaps it was myself whom I feared the most—that part of me who was a scared little boy that wanted safety. The part that never grew up. The part that alcohol anesthetized. This projection played out like a perfectly executed football pattern. I was the single "X" zig-zagging around the "O"s, hoping to avoid contact of any kind and to avoid being trampled and knocked down by others and their wants.

This kind of thinking still plays today. For example, last year I was looking forward to a certain road race I had been training for. For a year or so before this race, I had started to get to know some other local runners via social media—people who were experienced racers and were going to be at the race. They were very kind in sharing their knowledge and tips when it came to running. I got along with many of them. I knew what many of them looked like by their selfies, and they each showed their personalities. I was excited to be a small part of the community and I looked forward to meeting them in person at the race.

Then, my story started to play. "Why would people want to meet *you*?" "What do you have to offer?" "You barely know them." "You suck as a runner; they'll laugh at you." How typical of my ego to put me in a chokehold and squeeze out my air. I started to churn the machine of discontent. I rolled out the red carpet for my star storytellers to stroll out on.

When it came time to go to the expo the day before the race to pick up my racing bib, I avoided everyone. I took snapshots of some of the folks I had intended to meet (they were on stage doing talks), but I didn't approach them. I shrank back. I played small. I felt like an imposter. I recognized some other runners from their pictures, but I blended into the shadows. I turned myself inside out and slithered out of the venue.

Later on, I mentioned online about having been reluctant in meeting people, listing names, and I was met with some distance and even anger. "Why didn't you come up to us?" "What's wrong with you?" One guy even wrote, "Don't be a wiener." (For a week I used a picture of a hotdog as my avatar. Hello, my name is Passive-Aggressive.) I felt like I had let the others down, and I felt that I had let my lower self take the reins down to the dark, distant path. The path I had been down too many times.

Stay away and keep low on the radar—this is how I used to approach all of the other parts of my life. At the same time, all I ever wanted to do was to jump in and play ball with the other kids. I still do. My challenge is to be aware of my lone wolf tendencies and pray for the courage to change the things I can and push through the fears. What may be ferocious in effort for me is painfully easy for others. I am not them. I am me and I am learning to grow in a manner that reflects my history and my willingness to change.

When I feel the need to cocoon, to remove myself from the stream of other people's energy and to isolate myself, I can feel the weight of that solitary confinement. There is a difference between recharging or having alone time and disengaging and disconnecting. One gives me renewed energy while the other sucks the marrow from my bones. When I isolate myself, I either jump into the self-pity pool or I burst open and over-share with the nearest human being. I recall keeping one neighbour hostage in the produce aisle as I unloaded onto her countless uninvited minutiae of my life. The poor soul wanted to buy pomegranates and salad dressing and leave.

I need folks. I need you. I need family. I need neighbours. I need recovery people. I need runners. I need friends. I don't want to need them—let's be clear on this—but I need them. That's the new tale that I have been allowing the Creator to tell me, the one which my authentic self whispers to me when I pull away. He speaks to me through others, and they tell me that I am needed, too. Who would have thought that people needed me too? That goes against the lies of my 46 years on this planet. That flies in the face of my ego, which would rather be simmering in self-pity.

It's possible to change the stories we tell ourselves. It's possible and very likely to break out of our self-imposed prisons. It's possible to see that you are meant to be something greater than you imagine. It's possible to live in a new way, an authentic way and be a part of something greater than yourself.

Fun fact: Wolves travel in packs. They howl to assemble their group, to find a mate, to communicate their position and to show love.

They aren't so lone after all. That's just another bedtime story.

Spider in a Box

We sat in the bar. He observed my face as I stared at the bubbles rising in my beer glass. Joe was talking at a rate that rivaled Morse code in delivery and speed. I wasn't listening as much as I was just hearing him. Joe often overshared about himself in the hopes that I would take the bait and give a little back. This was one of those times. He plied me with liquor to encourage me to talk about my "feelings." I didn't bite. Drink, yes, but not bite. As we sat at the bar, my expression as empty as the glass I had just finished, and he finally quieted for a moment, he announced to no one in particular that I was a "spider in a box." An outcast in self-imposed exile. A recluse.

He was right. I asked for another drink.

***

"No man is an island…except for Freddy Madagascar."

That was one of my father's go-to lines. It's a dad joke. I didn't think much of it when I'd first heard it, but as the years have passed it's given me more than a few laughs. Looking back at my old life, the existence I had had with bottle in hand, I could see that the joke really was on me. I was that little island and I didn't even know it. I don't imagine poet John Donne saw it as a joke. Johnny-boy was diving into bell tolling and deeper thoughts. I was just diving into alcohol and deeper kegs.

Ask almost any alcoholic and they will admit to being isolated in one way or another. I was a secretive, closet drinker. I drank alone, too, Mr. Thorogood. Like many others, I drank alone to avoid the ever-increasing concerned looks of friends and family and to avoid their glares of judgment. I drank alone to box myself in a frail yet powerful mixture of alcohol, self-pity and anger. I drank alone because people just got in the way of a good thing and I needed more of the medicine to keep me going. Alcohol was the only way I got through the day.

In terms of comfort, bottles were my supply. People needed not apply.

Isolation isn't just a physical manifestation of where we are within. Not all alcoholics sit in their basements, drinking homemade beer that has gone off or downing sweet sherry in alleyways. Many can be found in barrooms and taverns. Many drink in lounges, in clubs, at parties, at cottages and at other getaways. Some drink while having morning baby play dates. Many drink before, during and after vacations with their partners and buddies. While many alcoholics may physically be with others, they are still isolated—mentally, emotionally and spiritually. We don't have to be hiding in some dingy cave, scratching out the days with dirty, cracked fingernails on cold stone to be isolated. We hide within ourselves and cast others aside, castaways on our own little island. We are the Freddy's of the world.

Isolating was a way that I could fulfill my self-propelled prophecy of not being wanted. It was a way of escaping within an escape. It was like hiding in a sack that was nestled in a vault, hidden under a labyrinth. When I isolated myself, I ensured that I couldn't be seen, which was one of my greatest fears. I was playing hide-and-seek, except that I didn't want anyone to seek me even though I so craved to be found.

Psychotherapist D.W. Winnicott once stated "It is a joy to be hidden but a disaster not to be found."[2] Except, in this case,

---

[2] Winnicot, D.W. 1963. Communicating and Not Communicating Leading to a Study of Certain Opposites.

I had a big part of me not wanting to be found, and then resented when no one came looking for me. That was how my sick mind operated. And then adding alcohol to the mixture fueled the delusion, fear and anger. Wax on, wax off. Keep it going, young Daniel.

Another aspect of my isolation was the feeling of ascendancy. In separating myself from others physically, I separated myself from others holistically. I was declaring to the world (or really, myself) that I was a much more advanced specimen of human. To mix among the plebes, minions and serfs of the planet meant that I was common, and for a man of my *obvious* intellectual prowess and superior *homo sapiens* status, I could not stand for such insipidness in my world. I could not be common because my ego just couldn't handle the throwing of the gauntlets like that. I was a man on the go, on the way up, didn't you know? I had plans to conquer all, including myself. To demonstrate that, I needed go to my quiet cavern and hatch grand schemes, to make known the injustices of my warped world and to get back at you. To do that I needed some space. I needed a place, mentally and physically, to recreate myself once again. I just needed room to breathe, and everyone was sucking in my precious air.

The more isolated I was, the more difficult it was to get back into the stream of life. There was something almost comforting about being self-imprisoned. It seemed like the only way to live. The natural, hard-wired instinct of connecting with others was at first dampened, then strangled out of me. I was able to relate less and less to others, to care less and less of others, and eventually, care less and less of myself. My grand plans were nothing more than tissue paper flitting about over white hot coals. They vaporized the more I drank. They crumbled as my cocoon cracked and caved in around me, hands still clutching to wet glass, face against cold tile, pain erupting from my very soul.

Isolation, like the alcohol and rage, was killing me. It was complicit in my deterioration.

Donne was right when he said that we were all interconnected. When he writes in his poem *No Man is an Island*, "Any man's death diminishes me because I am involved in mankind," he speaks of the fellowship of humanity. For me, it's about the fellowship of those who have crawled into dark spaces and know loneliness like no other, yet who have come out of the other side. Being in recovery has given me a sense of community that I've never experience before. Being surrounded by those who are on the spiritual path of wellness and self-discovery has been a lesson in humility and love. Being with like-minded people has given me the chance to understand the connection we have with one another, and to understand how bright and nourishing that connection is.

Taking the jump away from isolation was a leap of faith. It was letting go of what once served me for a very long time. It was finding my way into the collective arms of others. It was taking the action to sit with, share with, listen to and heal with others. It was keeping an open and teachable mind. It was challenging myself to reach out even when my lizard brain told me that I may get hurt.

What I have found in this practice is that it's not about being less than or better than, but about being right-sized, or equal to others. It's about feeling my way through the centre of myself through others and their breath, touch and speech. It's about plugging in. It's about getting off of the island of me and joining the continent of others.

The pull of isolation is still strong at times. I have learned the difference between keeping alone in a healthy way and isolating myself. The good news is that it doesn't take me long to get back in the slipstream of being with others. A simple call, a quick meeting or a hand out to someone in need and boom, I am back in the game. It's about the faith and conviction to open that box and to row away from the island. Reconnecting is just that simple, and just as rewarding.

.

Fearfulness – Faith

"He has not learned the lesson of life who does not every day surmount a fear."
~ **Ralph Waldo Emerson**

"To one who has faith, no explanation is necessary. To one without faith, no explanation is possible."
~ **Thomas Aquinas**

Painting Spaces

I am an introverted soul, which means I am more apt to sit quietly amongst the giants of gregariousness and soak in the ambiance rather than hold court amongst semi-strangers. But get me one-on-one and tickle me with a topic that wets my goat and my mouth fires off like an auctioneer after a triple espresso. It's like all of my words are exacting vengeance against the silence that preceded them. If it weren't for that pesky breathing part of our biology, I would probably skip that to get in an extra word or two. There is nothing wrong with being a little animated or excited about something, but I have certainly been more aware of how I can bombard myself and others with endless chatter when a good dose of not chatting can be just as useful and beneficial.

One evening, my wife and I went to see the Soweto Gospel Choir. It was a beautiful and powerful performance, with uplifting singing and music. They could hit huge highs and rumbling lows, and belt out when needed. What got my attention, for some reason, were the times when they held silence. There was a respectful restraint at times, inter-played with roving soft tones and hushed semiquavers. With all of the vocal majesty and power at their command, they sat in the silent moments. They said more there than they did when they raised their voices to the heavens.

I once read about how great musicians learn when to *not* play notes. They let the silence breathe and give a certain cadence to the music, like a counterpoint to give it texture. Orchestra conductor Leopold Stokowski, addressing a Carnegie Hall audience in 1967, mentioned that musicians paint their pictures on silence. I clutch onto this image as I sit back and think about how I am in this world, how I am with others and how I am with myself.

Painting silence. This is a tough call for someone who used every available empty spot to park his yap-a-mobile and vent toxic exhaust for everyone within range to suck in. Not pleasant. Silent spots were always tough for me growing up and even into early recovery. I couldn't sit properly with silence. It was threatening, it held me captive and it didn't allow me to compensate for the unease I felt. Silence was for churches, for temples and for those weirdos who meditated. Why have awkward silence when bellowing could edge that out easily and neatly?

In playing in the high school band, I learned all of the notes—whole, half, quarter, etc. I also learned about strange symbols that denoted rest points. Rest? Why rest? Why not sustain things, keep the ball rolling and get our funk on? It was useful when I first started playing, to give my novice woodwind jaw a break, but once I got past that I wanted to keep at it. I resented those breaks. I wanted to keep blowing that hot air.

It wasn't until my final year in band that I started to understand the reason for the rests, for the silence. In art, they speak of negative and positive space. Aspect ratios. Even in my culinary trade, when putting food on the plate in an artistic manner, we use those concepts of space and non-space. We use the rule of odd numbers. There has to be that negative, or silent, space to balance things out, to allow for the eye, ear, mind and spirit to equilibrate. To give dramatic pause and to allow the light of the non-being to shine.

For years, I was the horn that wouldn't stop trumpeting. I was the air raid siren that persisted even at the absence of any inherent danger. Or was there a real danger? That's important, because when I was drinking, everything was a danger or threat to me. Everything. How you looked at me, how you spoke to me, how you didn't speak to me, how you held your coffee when near me—everything was a threat against my well-being. So off I went like a sprinkler at the first whiff of smoke.

That's how I stumbled through life—yammering and barking my way through, afraid that if I shut off I would be overwhelmed not only by you, but by me. My thoughts of worthlessness, guilt, anger, and fear would bubble up and I would get swallowed. So, I drank away my fears and created a negative inner dialogue, a soundtrack so to speak, to drown out the drinking.

Keep talking so they don't see your pain, Paul. It doesn't matter who you talk to—the cat, the tree or the bald lady that lives across the street. Keep at it, keep blowing those pipes, keep that glass full, keep the lies and drama up, keep beating yourself up, keep blaring that death metal, keep the white noise on at night, keep the radio on full blast, keep keeping on.

Full noise. Full stop.

It wasn't the talking so much as it was the noise level. I matched the noise around me to the twisted, terrifying noise in my head. No silence or reprieve within meant no silence or reprieve without. The sheet music would be solid black with the amount of notes jammed on there. I couldn't find a rest stop even with a AAA map and GPS, because silence meant pain.

The turning point for me in finding the value of silence was about a year into my recovery. I was still uncomfortable with the idea of silence. What I learned was that it was in the rest notes, the silence, that I was able to process things. I was able to just be and to take in the moment. I learned to actually occupy my mouth by breathing and not forming useless consonants and vowels. I learned to listen for the first time in my life. Coming from a serial interrupter like me, this was gold. Instead of thinking of what I was going to say next, and forming that lovely Oscar speech in my head, I just forced myself to listen. It's something that I have to continually foster in myself.

Improving on that silence brought me to a place of now being one of those aforementioned weirdo meditation dudes. Sitting in stillness doesn't necessarily mean burning incense and chanting. Not at all. It can, but doesn't have to. I sometimes sit in the park and just gaze out at the children playing, the people skating, the people hanging with their dogs or the wind rustling the leaves. Other times I am running, I focus on my breath or on the sound of my feet smacking against the pavement. There is a rhythm and pace that brings me to a deeper place.

This has brought me many rewards in my interactions with others. Working with others has also taught me the value of shutting my trap and taking things in, as is. Learning to not play the notes. Painting silence. Taking in what others say, hearing their own pauses in speech, listening for what they aren't saying and reading between the lines—the things I would miss if I were using my own words to plug in the holes of silence. Tapping into the unspoken brings me some greater clarity in my own inner landscape and in connecting with others.

"Sometimes the best solution is doing nothing at all," a friend of mine said recently. I understood what he meant. To carry that further, sometimes the best thing to do is to say nothing. Sometimes people want to be heard and nothing else (I learned that one from my wife), so chirping about this and that, giving advice and offering solutions is not what they want. Sometimes I just need to sit in their pain and stay quiet. Keep painting.

It's the balance of said and not-said that anchors me to a sense of well-being and connection with others. When I stop my ego from wanting to be in the spotlight, when I filter the noise from the necessary, when I shed the shawl of showmanship, when I take in the moment and don't soil it with unnecessary verbiage, then I take in more of the negative space and take in more breathing room.

Sometimes I just need to put my instrument onto my lap, breathe and listen the music around me.

Leap

I saw them the other day.

They looked like all of the other ones I've seen before, and they still break my heart.

I didn't see them the day before on my ride home from work, but there they were now.

Fresh flowers. Teddy bears. Bright red ribbons flowing in the wind. They were all attached to the bridge's railing posts, marking where someone stood and stared at the traffic below, taking in their last few breaths. Perhaps they knew that they would end, soon.

I feel the need to stop whenever I find ad hoc memorial sites. Whether if it's on a run, a bike ride or a stroll through the park, I stop and look. I don't touch anything.

I looked over the railing and wondered if they felt anything at the end. Was it better than what was shredding them up inside? Did they tear up, perhaps tapping into that small part of them which knew there was perhaps another way out? Or was it too late? Had they numbed out long enough that it was a matter of follow through and physics by that point?

I don't think of these things in a morbid way. I think about them because I know I was in a very dark place many times in my own life. I know that feeling of wanting to shut it down permanently. I understand that need to not be in pain any more. These feelings were strongest when I got sober, when I felt that I couldn't live with the drink nor could I live without it. I figured it would be best not to live at all. It was too hard.

What I understand now is that it wasn't so much that I wanted to die, but that I just didn't want to live. There's a considerable difference. Numbing myself with alcohol to the point of oblivion was the closest I could get to dying on a regular basis. I killed my spirit with more spirit. I drowned my emotions until they choked. I bled my soul out so that I could maybe make it through the day. I crushed myself under the weight of my own twisted wreckage. Offing myself one ounce at a time was a suicide-by-installment plan which seemed to suit me like a tight coffin.

Moving through the struggle of both wanting to die and wanting to live was one of the toughest times in my journey. I had no choice but to make a massive shift in my thinking and perceptions of myself and the world. If I wanted to stick around, I had to pitch the idea of easy outs, like booze and suicide, and get down to the brass tacks of cleaning house and facing my fears. There were many times I raged against myself, others and God. But I kept at it, because I knew that my life needed to be more than just a stain to be scraped off of the street, sandblasted and sanitized from the earth.

One ironic notion about the journey is reflected in the Prayer of St. Francis: "It is in dying that we are born to eternal life." In order for me to live, to break out of my death spiral, I needed to die many times. I needed my ego to break, crumble and fall to the ground. I needed to let go of all of the things which were suffocating me. I needed to lay waste to the spiritual toxins clogging me up. Killing my old self was what I needed to break through and start anew. The plunge always comes from within and cascades outwards.

When I look back at the greatest jumps in my growth, they came on the heels of the dying embers of flames that once threatened to consume me. They came from gathering everything within and moving through the darkness. It was never easy, but the outcome always brought me closer to the

Creator, to my authentic self. I felt renewed and rejuvenated. I never liked the pain, but I knew that I was better off having gone through it.

So as I look at the makeshift commemoratives wrapped around steel poles, I wonder how that person would have been today if they had stepped back and allowed themself to walk through the darkness rather than make the final sacrifice. I wonder what wisdom would have welled up from their pain. I wonder what scars they would have shown.

In the end, the most painful and yet rewarding and liberating leap is that of faith. As long as I keep hold of that faith, I know that I can soar.

(The next day I rode past the place where the flowers, teddy bears, and bright red ribbons flowed the night before, and everything was gone.)

The Pity Patter of Self Defeat

> *"Self-pity is easily the most destructive of the non-pharmaceutical narcotics; it is addictive, gives momentary pleasure and separates the victim from reality."*
> ~ **John Gardner**

Self-pity.

The word itself (or compound word, at least) alone sounds desolate. The hyphen plays for dramatic pause. Looks-wise, the hyphen resembles a metal bar between two heavy weights, a barbell that I can clean and jerk to build up my ego even further and to tone up my self-centred thoughts of despair. It's a workout for the lower self, the one who likes to play victim. And no one likes to play victim more than the active alcoholic.

If you asked me why I drank, I would scrawl out my grudge list on a piece of paper the length of a returns lineup on Boxing Day, resplendent with the names of people, institutions and principles that irked me. This revengeful list acted as a blueprint for my blaming and, eventually, for the bottle passing my lips. How dare it be my fault that I drank? If you felt like I did when I didn't drink, you'd drink too. I was a man who had a constant chalk mark around his body as he walked around. A neon sign flashed on my chest: Chump.

Like alcohol, self-pity was something I wallowed in and swallowed straight up, undiluted. Self-pity was part and parcel of my alcoholism. Like depression and anxiety, self-pity was part engine, part exhaust of the vehicle. Self-pity helped to drive the vehicle, and yet it was a by-product of driving the vehicle. It was a twisted ouroboros, a toxic circle of living that fed upon itself. The more I felt sorry for myself, the more I drank, and the more I drank, the more I felt sorry for myself. Poor me, poor me, pour me another drink, as the saying goes. That saying goes for good reason. Staying caught up in the moment, like a needle on a skipping record, I was in a rut that I couldn't jar into moving. And even if I did, I would find a way to get right back into the trough of pity. Pour me another drink, barkeep.

While I found self-pity to be a wonderful companion in my active alcoholic days, I never saw it for the nefarious creature that it would grow up to be. It became a relentless beast. Self-pity came easily to me. I didn't have to struggle to feel sorry for myself. It was one of those things that I could tee up and crank out of the ballpark, every single time. Self-pity was a security blanket. Self-pity was a favourite pet to whom I fed anger and fear in kibble-sized pieces. Self-pity was my "go to" when alcohol was or wasn't working. Self-pity gave me an identity, printed on a business card in bold and large font: Paul, Victim.

I never understood why self-pity was seen as such a big deal. So what if I was down on myself a bit? So what if I kicked myself while I was on the ground and thought less of myself? So what if I couldn't count one good grace in my life? I wasn't hurting anyone, right? So what was the big deal? The deal is, kitten, that self-pity is dangerous grounds for a sensitive soul like me.

I may not have been addicted to self-pity, but I did find it intoxicating. I find that this holds true even today. If and when I choose (yes, I choose to wallow in self-pity), it's exhilarating. It's a dip into the forbidden and lost sea. It swells my head and closes off my eyes and ears. It hardens my heart and sends me into some hookah-laced trance, complete with psychedelic white rabbit trips and a kaleidoscope of groovy colours. Black, black and grey, namely. When I am immersed in self-pity, everything floats away. I am the only one there. I am grounded to nothing and my thinking reflects that. That's the allure of self-pity—nothing, and yet all *me*. It cuts me off from the Sunlight of the Spirit. I am once again bubble wrapped up in me.

Self-pity is fear and self-centredness ripped on steroids. When I feel sorry for myself, I am fearful of something. This may sound odd at first. If I am scared of something, why would I sit in self-pity? "Oh woe is me" is my anesthetic to things that lure out fear. The way it works is this: When I am frozen in fear, I react by convincing myself that there is no choice in the matter. I am fated to be in some particular situation that I can't change. This is because I fear making that change. Fear comes down to two thoughts: I may lose something I already have, or I may not get something I want. So, if I am afraid of making a change in my life or environment, then I justify doing nothing by getting into a place of victimization. In that victimization, I am no longer in the sphere of gratitude. I lose perspective. I start to see the negative in myself. I start to see the perceived pointlessness in the situation. Self-esteem gets trampled on and I find myself dropping down the ladder of spirituality. I head to the basement, where the creepy and furry creatures make their home.

Self-pity also makes me of no use to others. When I am wrapped up in self, I don't see you. You don't exist. All of a sudden I forget all of the things that I should be grateful for. I can't help you in any way because I am so entrenched in my own filth that I am immobilized. The more I get wrapped up in myself, the more I stay wrapped up in myself. Sounds familiar, yes? My alcoholism worked in exactly the same way. My drinking wore the same shiny clothes to coax me into a dull shell of me. I lose.

Self-pity has no rewards other than pulling me deeper into self-pity. It cuts me off from others, from you and from the Creator. It's like pulling a thread on a finely knit sweater and watching it unravel, stitch by beautiful stitch. It's like sitting in a box and breathing your own filthy exhalation over and over again. It's like poking yourself in the eye hoping to help you see better. It's a wasted process and a way to dull the roar without dealing with the lion.

As my default, it's not always easy to shift gears, but I am learning to veer left when I normally dive right, feigning downward when the uppercut is jutting towards my jaw. I am learning to polka and not dive into the mosh pit where boots scrape against my temples. This is one of the greatest challenges I have on my own journey. The pull is often great, and like the drink it always tries to find a way to bring me back to it. Sure, I won't get pulled over for having too much self-pity in my system, but that is no reason to indulge.

My room for growth is limitless, as it is for all. Our ability to break through and get past what holds us down is in our capacity and limits. I have many tools at my fingertips, including prayer, fellowship with others and meditation, and it's my choice whether I use them or not. I am not powerless against self-pity. The choice is mine whether I side with bleakness or gratitude. Darkness or brightness. Pain or love. Ego or selflessness. Self-pity or self-esteem. When I move away from the business of self-pity, I slip into the motion of gratitude.

Gratitude is the antidote to the poison of self-pity.

I am ready to throw my old business cards out. Perhaps I will get new ones: Paul. Child of God. Extraordinaire.

The Place Where I Met Myself

I navigated my bike through the slush and snow, reflecting on another day at work as I rode home. It was late. The temperature had dipped below zero long before the sun went down. As I hit the halfway point of my ride, there was a deep pull in my chest, a ringing in my mind and a compulsion driving me—I needed to stop. Something in me was compelling me to sit. Just sit. I knew that to fight it or to ignore it would be pointless—I needed to be off the road. I had had this kind of feeling before and I knew I couldn't ignore it. I was approaching a parkette—a little patch of grass no longer than a few bus lengths, nestled between a parking lot and some office buildings. There were benches littered about. I pulled over and laid my bike against the nearest post.

Before I could even finish sitting down, I felt arising from me a wave of tears that was both unexpected and unwavering. I sat, hands cradling my cheeks, as the tears ran out in waves, each sob deeper and stronger than the last. As each wave receded, I heard something come from within me. It was a tiny voice that got louder every moment. "You are where you need to be. I love you. I forgive you." Over and over these words came to me, a mantra of sorts, all in between the sobs. I couldn't understand what was happening to me.

I sat for several minutes, reciting and weeping, speaking and listening, as the air warmed around me. As I sat there, wiping my face, I looked up in front of me. Two slight trees, with bare limbs looking like broken glass against the faint light of the city, stood before me. Their branches were lightly entwined, like lovers grazing fingertips. In between them stood a lamppost, its light blazing.

As I stared at those trees, I started to realize why I was there. Sitting there, I felt something that I hadn't really felt before. I felt that everything was going to be alright. I always knew intellectually that I would be "fine," but it was the first time that I felt it in my body. The tears I shed were the last vestiges of the war I had waged against myself long ago for not being the person I was meant to be, for a life that went astray from my drinking and for hating myself for all of those years. And then something broke, like a fever. As the waves finally started to part and pull away, I started to feel a peace that I hadn't felt in a long while. It wasn't like I just had a good cry and felt better. This was more profound.

I had finally forgiven myself. I had given myself permission to forgive myself, for me. Through my internal work and through cleaning my side of the street, metaphorically, I had been forgiven by others and I had forgiven them in return, but I had held out on myself. I always knew that I was the last hurdle, but I didn't know how to do overcome it. I had had no idea. But, for some reason, time allowed the dam to burst. I was finally free of my own hand striking me down. I could look at myself now and realize that I was not a bad man. I wasn't bad. My alcoholism tried to tell me that I was, with my ego riding shotgun, and in the end it was all untrue. Truth, my truth, shone through that night.

I looked at those trees touching. I noticed that each tree branched out in different directions. They were like me—my two selves, old and new, were coming to meet. The light between them was a conduit, a bridge between the two. It was like the old me had gone as far as it could and was passing through some energy or field to allow the new me to continue the journey. I had met myself. And this place where I met myself was not marked on any conventional map; it was in a little park, but it was way out in another place, deep inside me. The place where I met myself was full of love. I could be at peace.

I soon felt it was time to go. There hadn't been any sounds other than the light wind, but the voices of people passing by and cars sweeping past invaded the silence. I picked up my bike and jumped on. Before I left, I realized one more thing. To get to the parkette, I had ridden over tire tracks and footprints. I had arrived at the place where I met myself by treading where others had been, by following a path that had been laid out before me. But, as I clicked into low gear and started off, I noticed a clean sheet of snow beneath and ahead of me. My tire tracks were the first to crunch the snow. I was charting my own path, my own journey. I was on my way home, from the place where I met myself.

Resistance – Surrender

"On the other side of resistance is the flow."
~ **Guy Finley**

"The greatness of a man's power is the measure of his surrender."
~ **William Booth**

The Sentencing and the Veil

Friday came with an undertow of calm anxiety. The boys still needed to eat their breakfast, to change and to walk to school. My oldest threw snowballs at me as we made our way down to their classes. The little one laughed with every square hit. We raced the neighbours down the street to the school.

As we walked, glided and jogged, I thought about not trying to think. I popped Serenity Prayers like candies. I breathed God in and breathed fear out. I used visualization techniques and I listened to the crunch and squeak of snow underneath each foot as I treaded carefully around icy patches.

This was the last day of a trial that had lasted just slightly longer than my own sobriety. This was just another day in the court system. Another day, another verdict. Another goof who did something really stupid and is paying for it. More paper to push. I knew that today was going to be the last day, barring a calamity of sorts. All arguments had been exhausted. Both sides were weary from presenting their cases. The ruling had already been handed down: Guilty. The only item left on the docket was my sentencing.

* * *

"Wow, you're in a good mood," my wife said as I entered the car.

Our friend was driving my wife and me down to the courthouse. I had texted our friend Marah on Thursday and told her not to worry about coming. It was going to be quick, and it wasn't worth her long drive from the suburbs. She insisted. That was Marah. She and my wife met and worked in a bar a long time ago. Little did my wife know then that she would be accompanying her booze hound husband to court to find out what the system would mete out to him for his ugly transgression.

"Did you get rest?" Marah asked.

"Not getting rest wouldn't change anything that happens today," I replied.

My mental state was filed under "It is what it is." That's often a good place for my mind to be. It doesn't allow for free falling or grandiose schemes. Left to my own devices, I will create scenarios that would make George Orwell or Sylvia Plath look like optimists. I will envision the utter pit of despair or conceive flights of fancy and fantasy that are equally as unrealistic. I had already done that a few weeks ago before the ruling—images of me kicking my heels as a free man. The ink ran out on those sketches, so the best I could do was just be in the moment and not let the dog off of the leash, so to speak.

We drove and talked about traffic, *Little House on the Prairie* and parenthood.

* * *

Here's the thing about alcoholism: It takes you down twists and turns you never thought possible. I could always turn to someone else and say "See? I am not as bad as him. I still have control over things." I could then move on. I justified and rationalized while I poisoned my mind, body and soul with pollutant in a bottle. I was never as bad as that guy on TV shotgunning Lysol. Now, that's bad. It's amazing how far down the scale we can slide. It's just a matter of when we want to jump off.

I thought of this as Marah, my wife and I walked past the people on their way to work, with their half-eaten bagels getting cold in the northern wind, cellphones gripped and coffees steaming up the sidewalks. If they knew my story, if they knew me, would they have pointed at me like I did at the

Lysol dude? Would those men and women already thinking of after work drinks, or those who have a little nip of something in their coffees at 9:45 am point at me and have said, "See? I am not as bad as him. I still have control over things"?

This whole deal wasn't about my alcoholism, per se, but of the consequences of my alcoholism, and those are two different things. I certainly was an alcoholic before the consequences started to pile up. I certainly was an alcoholic before I could admit it to myself. I certainly was an alcoholic then, as I am now. But, what was going on the day of the sentencing, and the countless days before that, wasn't an indictment of me or my alcoholism. It was of what my alcoholism brought me to do.

* * *

My lawyer once warned me that there is always a chance of getting bed bugs at the court. Posh New York City hotels and opera houses had them, so why not a downtown metropolis courthouse? Especially a courthouse located in a nondescript building above a coffee shop and a Winners. The courthouse sees all sorts, including guilty-type sorts like me.

After spending enough time wandering the hallways, I was able to discern between the suits—which ones were cops, which ones were lawyers and which ones were like me in ill-fitting, off-the-rack, cheap suits. One day I had a guy ask me if

I was a lawyer. I wanted to tell him that I too was just another contestant on the wheel of fortune, but instead I simply laughed and pointed him towards the counsellor's office.

Sitting on the maybe-infested-with-bed-bugs benches that Friday, we waited for my lawyer's representative, since my lawyer could not attend. My parents, my wife, Marah and my sponsor James were there. I brought James my copy of *Sermon on the Mount* by Emmet Fox. It was a book I knew he would like, being where he was on his own spiritual journey. As I handed him the book, the representative showed up and we marched into the body of the court. If there is anything I can say about the court system, amidst the general tedium and long delays, is that it starts right on time. Having borne witness to many other legal and judicial proceedings in my time there, they move at a quick hustle. In and out. Yes or no. Guilty or not guilty. Next.

The court was busier than I had seen it before. Clients were brought up before the judge and hustled to other court rooms. Arrangements were made for new dates and petitions were pitched. One man pleaded guilty to credit card identity theft. The court took an early recess, as they needed to find the old prosecutor. I spoke to James in the meantime, and told him that I was ready to move on and to not have this over my head any longer. He told me that he had had that cloud over his head for ten or eleven years—whenever he got out of one "jackpot," he would get pinched for something else. I told him that if I got jail time my lawyer would ask for house arrest. James told me his experience with that as well, then we talked about the book for a few minutes.

The judge returned and I sat down.

* * *

The judge did what judges do in these rulings: read out all of the facts, what the prosecutor brought to the table and the defense's arguments.

I was still not used to hearing the objective, hard-nosed facts of that day. The amount I drank. The picking up of my son from day care. The readings when I was caught and asked to blow. The 911 calls about my driving. It's never easy to have it all put on public record. Then again, I made it public record years ago when I did what I did. This wasn't one of those lazy, pathetic drunks in my basement. Well, let me correct that. *All of my drunks were pathetic.*

I heard the sniffling behind me. If it was difficult for me to hear at times, it was devastating for my own family and friends to hear it. My wife was doing her best not to cry. My lawyer's representative leaned over to me at one point and said, "Keep a poker face, no matter what." Well, that was a part of the plan. I couldn't see myself dropping down like I got hit by a sniper and floundering about, nor could I see myself jumping on the desk and doing a jig. Royal flush face.

As the judge kept reading, she continued to look at me. I heard what she said, word for word, and yet at the same time I was outside of myself, watching as detached as the court reporter. This wasn't caused by disinterest (I was quite interested, believe me), nor apathy. This was to remove my mind from attachment to just be in the moment. To allow the Sunlight of the Spirit to place-hold me. To be free of thoughts no matter the outcome. To allow the ribbon to unfold as it would.

As the ribbon unspooled, the judge stopped for a moment and asked me to rise. And I did.

* * *

A few days before the sentencing, my wife and I were in the car. My wife, of course, was driving. We were passing some trees along the highway and a vista of the nearby bridge overlooking the Don River. The bridge was covered with a wire cage called the Luminous Veil, which it's not so much an artistic piece (it is, in a way) as it is a suicide prevention installation. Many have decided to end their lives from that bridge. During construction of the Luminous Veil, there were tales of men and women jumping between the construction workers as the labourers pieced together wires. I have seen someone attempt suicide after the Veil was finished. People are determined when they are in the darkest places. We'll fight through anything when it comes to seeking oblivion or the final way out. I could relate because there were times I would have crawled over broken glass to get the relief that only a bottle could give. There are countless stories of what addicts have done to get their next fix, their next high or their next buzz, or to do whatever it took to keep up a lie. I certainly have mine.

I told my wife that I was going to give her the phone number of my boss at work, just in case. I couldn't find his business card in my wallet, so I told her I would get it later. There was silence in the car for a while, and then my wife told me that I had really thrown her off by saying what I did. Up until then, we had had the unwritten, unspoken pact of staying positive, of not even going to that place of "what if." And I had broken it in a footloose moment of practicality.

"You don't realize the impact you have on others in what you say," she said, wiping her eyes.

I apologized, and realized she was right. I was so used to living a life where I thought I didn't matter and where my words were meaningless, because my life had felt like that. I was used having a crushed spirit and thinking, "What did it matter that I broke a promise? What did it matter what came out of my mouth or not?" Like those people who looked over at the lush foliage surrounding the Don River before they plunged from the bridge, I felt so often that my existence held no significance to me or those in my life.

My wife once told me that in my alcoholic days I robbed people of *me*. I robbed people of the experience of me, because I was so self-absorbed and self-loathing.

My words do have meaning, because I have meaning. Not in an egotistical manner, but in a human manner.

I put my wallet away and didn't think about work anymore.

* * *

The sentence came down: no incarceration, but hefty fines. Parole for 18 months. Courses to attend and other alcohol-related treatments to comply with.

I could easily say that I was doing cartwheels inside, but I wasn't. It was still in "it is what it is" mode, as I let myself be that day. Having said that, I was relieved beyond measure. My wife and I didn't have to explain to our children why their Papi wasn't around on weekends. I didn't have to upset my work schedule. I didn't have to make additional plans with others for child care. Papi would be home.

There were the grim reminders that my actions needed reaction, and while I didn't have to sit in a cell there were still some big consequences. I was told that there could be an appeal by the prosecution, for which they needed 30 days. I planned on quietly counting those days out. As we convened outside of the courtroom, with hugs and kisses, handshakes and restrained smiles, I felt a great weight off of my shoulders. I looked around and wondered how long the weight would go on for some of the other people there. I recognized the same dejected and surprised faces that I once had. I saw in others the feeling that things would never get better.

My parents, wife and Marah left, leaving me with James. The lawyer's representative left soon after. James and I talked about computers, as he was getting one for the first time. I told him to call me if he ever needed help with it. He promised me he would, as he got up and left. I sat on the maybe-infested-with-bed-bugs bench, in my cheap suit, alone. I sat for a few minutes in an attempt to take it all in and to slowly turn the release valve. It was noon. The boys needed dinner, so I had to start on that. I also had some calls to make.

Life goes on. Even when people are jumping to their death while you're working, life goes on. It has to. That is what it was meant for. And I had a second one that was handed to me.

Handing Over the Keys

I would never admit to being a control freak, but I often dressed up as someone who looked like a control freak. I still can be one if I don't watch my spiritual P's and Q's (Pride and un-Quenched ego). I was a very busy man, playing God. It couldn't be that difficult, could it? I just had to rearrange the entire universe at every given sub-atomic level and mold it around my warped and twisted way of thinking. I was cramming square pegs into round holes using all the tools at my bloodied fingertips—intimidation, gaslighting, coercion, self-pity, charm and that old standby workhorse, dishonesty. I mollified, manipulated and used *Beetlejuice*-type trickery to get my way. I needed and wanted people to understand that there was only one way of doing things—mine—and any other way was an abomination of rational thought. In other words, you were an idiot if you crossed me, and I made sure to let you know that in my glorious passive-aggressive ways.

I was a lot of fun to be with, as you can imagine.

I was a nice guy. Really, ask around. I wasn't controlling. I wasn't that jealous, need-a-restraining-order type of control monster. I was the type who pervaded your space and psyche in *slow* time. I dismissed your intuition, your feelings and your thoughts. I underplayed the value of you. I inflated my own currency. It was a quiet coup, complete with smiles and back pats.

I had no interest in changing, even when it was in my best interest. When someone suggested I try something different, I dug my heels in deeper. I recall having more than one meltdown when my views were challenged. One day in particular, I was on my knees, railing against my wife, beating the ground with my fists and asking why it was that *I* always had to be the one to change and no one else had to. Cue the swelling music and camera close-up. Oh, the melodrama. The fact was that I was having a hissy fit a three-year-old would have been proud of. It was pure comedy, but I wasn't laughing then. I felt threatened and my pride and ego went into full frontal assault.

There is an expression used in recovery circles: "My best thinking got me here." This usually references one's presence at a 12-step meeting. It's a regular acknowledgement that we never had the answers. We had thought that we did, but we were wailing at that piñata in the dark, never getting our festive goods. What we got was pain. I couldn't manage my own life, let alone others. It was a cosmic joke. The inevitable backlash in trying to usurp the universe from doing its divine job.

I felt that handing over control in any way was a sign of weakness. I needed control because I felt out of control. I needed control because I carried fears of abandonment and rejection. If I could control you, you wouldn't leave me. I needed control because I felt it was the only way I could be seen. I needed control because my ego told me I was better than you. I needed control because the reality was that my self-esteem was threadbare and I needed something, anything, to make me feel like a human. With control came the weight of my own expectations, and the crushing disappointments that inevitably happened.

Relinquishing control was one of the most difficult and rewarding shifts I have made in this spiritual journey. When I released control to the Creator (if you're playing 12-step bingo, dab Step 3 here), I found myself off the hook. I no longer needed to be the One any more. I no longer needed to exercise every molecule of sheer will to shape the world to conform to my selfish needs. Once I made that decision, I knew that things would take on another complexion.

It's not that I was going to lie in bed all day and let the world pass me by. I still had to be an active participant in the hamster wheel of life. This wasn't a passive position. What I was doing was just handing over the keys to the shop to the Higher Power. That was it. If my life was a store until then, I had turned it upside down. The shelves were in disarray, the place stank, it was unclean and no one wanted to visit. There was an "Under New Management" sign taped up over the front door. I was taking direction from Him. I still had to sweep up, restock, clean the toilets and do the daily maintenance of the place. I wasn't playing video games in the back with my feet up on the counter. I still had to take action. The difference was that my will was now aligned with the New Employer.

I was no longer stressing over who came in. It didn't matter what they wanted, what they thought of the shop, what they were wearing, etc. I was just there to be of service. I wasn't there to tell them what to buy or what to do with themselves. I was courteous and helpful, and I made sure that they felt welcome. That was it. Everything else was not in my control nor was it my concern. What I found was that the business of living my life as a child of God rather than as an orphan of my own world-making had phenomenal amounts of freedom. I had breathing room.

Having the trust to let go is a test of faith. When I have faith in a greater power, I am able to relieve myself of being the *majordomo* of my affairs. I can focus on the things that are of use to others and myself. I can be a present father, husband and friend. I have space to grow and develop. I can pass on what has been given to me. When I start to feel out of sorts, it's often because I know that in some way I am trying to wrest that control back. When I consciously or unconsciously try to tip the scales in my favour or force situations which aren't meant to be, I am back at the watchtower, trying to pick people off with my selfishness and self-centredness. In fact, I only shoot myself in the foot.

Trust, faith, surrender—these are interwoven together. Without them, I am floundering at the feet of my own doom-making machine. I am back under old management. Or in my case, mismanagement. Handing over the keys has been vital in unlocking myself from the bondage of self, and I will keep sweeping the shop and washing the windows. It's always great to see the light shine in on clean floors.

Compliant to Verbal Commands

It happens all the time in war movies: the enemy is surrounded and there is little chance of victory. The outnumbered soldiers wave a white flag as they shuffle out of their hiding spot, into an open and vulnerable space. The victors close in, guns cocked and ready. The defeated soldiers then place their firearms in front of them, kneel and interlace their hands behind their heads or backs. They keep their neck bent down. There is no chance of attack—they have fully submitted to the next act, an act out of their control. They have fully surrendered.

When I was arrested for drinking and driving, I had to give in to the officers. I had no choice. My hands were outstretched for them to see—no tricks, no weapons. I had to put down my excuses, my usually sparkling manipulative patter and my dignity, and allow them to put my hands behind my back. I was restrained in tongue and mobility. I forfeited my rights to wiggle out of the situation. I was surrounded. I had to fully submit to the next act, an act out of my control. I listened and took direction, and I was compliant to verbal commands. I had fully surrendered.

Until that moment, I was never truly compliant to others. I may have smiled and nodded, but my passive-aggressive, or just plain aggressive, actions masked the truth—I needed to always be the victor. Everything in sight was an enemy target. I scoured the landscape to identify every high tower and advantageous sight line my opponents may have had. I engaged in low ground fire whenever I could. I lobbed damaging verbal hand grenades whenever I felt threatened, or even as a preventative measure. I looked for signs of attack in everyone I met. I never let my guard down. I didn't trust others because I didn't trust myself.

Life was about hand-to-hand combat. Everything came at a price, and I would not be undermined by land mines. I struck first just in case someone was planning a sneak attack. I sensed that anyone I came into contact with was after something or wanted to take something from me. It was full shields up, prepare the Romulan cloaking device, and have all weapons ready to fire on my command. It was tiring to always be in war mode. It was mentally, physically and emotionally draining to be on watch at all times. There was no relief soldier to give me a break on the lookout shift. I was a lone wolf on the prowl.

Ego is a forceful but greatly flawed general and commander-in-chief. It can drop bombs on the enemy with no thought of the shrapnel it catches itself. It doesn't care about right or wrong, in the social or ethical sense. It is just *right* no matter the circumstances. Even when wrong, it will assign blame like one assigns kitchen duty to a lowly private. Ego will not allow itself to lose its status and stripes because of poor decisions. To the ego, any action or inaction is justified. It is the Great I Am; it just *is*. I let my ego rule with ruthless efficiency. It kept me at DEFCON 1 at all times. It was *War Games*. Do you want to play a game?

My need to be right and to be a step ahead of the game put me at odds against the feelings I had in the rare quiet times — the feelings of knowing that I was very, very wrong. There was friction between the way I conducted myself and way I felt I should have been living my life. My ego always won out. It directed me against those stirrings in my soul and I just battened down the hatches that much more. War paint and pig heads on sticks, on the double.

As my drinking worsened, the consequences of it began to pile up like shell casings. I found myself screaming out foxhole prayers more often. I couldn't get myself out of the crossfire of my own fears, resentments and anger. I was trapped with the thought of dying a painful death. At this point I was alone, adrift and choking on the blood of my own victimhood. I could no longer hole up and keep my sanity. The fight had long gone out of me, and I knew there was only one thing left for me to do. The general would not be happy, but my life depended one single act: surrender.

My act of surrender was simple yet significant. It was both painful and liberating. My surrender came through the small crack in my ego. A crack small enough that I could see light's freedom shining through. I had to let go of all of my preconceived notions of who I was. I had to concede to my innermost self that I was not a soldier of fortune, a Rambo-type person pitted against the world. What I came to see was that I was really at war with myself, with whom I thought I was and with the pretenses I had put up.

I had to lay down my weapons—ego, pride, anger, resentments, dishonesty, etc.—and come down to my knees. I had to ask for help and show that I didn't have the answers. I clasped my hands together, not behind my head, but in prayer. True prayer. Not hovering-over-the-toilet-bowl-please-God-get-me-out-of-this-one prayer. But sincere and genuine prayer. The prayer of a desperate man who knew that the war was over.

Surrender doesn't mean weakness. Surrender doesn't display ineptitude. Surrender doesn't paint us with a brush of failure. Surrender shows strength. It shows courage. It demonstrates true humility. When I cease fighting everything and everyone, I am at peace. I am in a place divorced from the casualties of war and displacement. I stand in the quiet of the desolate neutral zone. I can focus my energy and light on the process of healing, rather than harming. Surrender shows a higher wisdom in letting go of the relentless battle, especially ones which don't serve us.

I learned to be compliant to suggestions that others offered. I learned to not only listen to others, but also to the heart within my heart, where my authentic self resides. I learned to keep a teachable mind, and to resist the urge to pick up my old weapons whenever I felt threatened. And by threatened, I speak of perceived threats, because my mind will create false scenarios of incoming missiles when there are none. My spiritual and mental practice is to decipher between my reality and the true reality. It's fact-checking to a higher degree.

There are times when I need to speak up, to clear my throat and to lay down or enforce boundaries. There are instances when I need to engage in battles small and large. I am not a door mat. So, the challenge is in knowing when to light up that fire and when to stand down. I can be vigilant and proactive, and still be in a surrendered state. I take the actions, but I leave the outcome to my Higher Power. I can be a swashbuckling swordsman when I need to be, but I still accept that I can't control everything around me except for my own actions and reactions.

Surrender has been my greatest coup.

Closing Windows

I always wanted more in my life. More stuff. More distractions. More of what I could jam down my life's throat like a sausage machine, and still have some leftover sludge for pâté. I wanted more attention, more love, more hand holding, more freedom, more strength, more drama, more booze, more, more, more. If I didn't have it, I wanted it. If I had it, I wanted the next big thing. I am not talking material stuff, per se—I never had much interest in cars, houses or fancy clothes—although it did come into play at times. I just wanted to fill up inside and not think about anything. I wanted to horde my way into oblivion or happiness, whichever came first. And when the happiness wasn't sticking around, I chose to make oblivion my new roommate, rent-free. Little did I know that oblivion came with a price.

I needed to be treated extraordinarily to feel ordinary. A simple wave across the street wasn't good enough for me. I needed you to beat traffic like one did in *Frogger*, bow before me and throw blood red rose petals at my feet for me to just feel that I was acknowledged. And that was just with my mail carrier or an acquaintance. Living in a fantasy world like that, imagine the disconnection I had between my mind, my feelings and my expectations of people. When I didn't get that kind of attention (and why would I?), I threw an internal hissy fit and drank *at* you. I became indignant and angry and wanted to punish you by destroying my body, mind and spirit, in one ounce increments. What "more" I didn't get from you, I found in the bottle. The bottle always had "more."

When the gates opened like they did at the Battle of the Morannon, a lot of other orcs came for the ride—fear, anger, resentment, dishonesty, etc. I sure got what I wanted—everything. And everything brought me barrels of pain. It rippled out and affected everyone in my life. Being full of this negativity distracted me from the pain of looking at me. It was easy to look away from my lack of self-esteem and confidence when I was creating crisis after crisis, when I was involved in other people's business and when I was drowning in my own shame, vomit and vodka. I didn't have to look in the mirror when I was consumed with mayhem, when I obsessed over inconsequential things or when I got worked up about something that was none of my business. I was the drunk male Gladys Kravitz, but I wouldn't have admitted it. Despite all of the filibuster filler in my inner life, I still felt empty.

I choked on all of the vitriol I stored up. I no longer had a sense of who I was anymore or of where I was in the world. Like an aging magician, my tricks had worn thin and fooled nobody. What were once my defenses now attacked and plagued me. I was swarmed by the Four Horsemen, now backed up by their posse of the Seven Deadly Sins. That's six five, no jive, in craps. They win. I lose. My ego, my pride and my way of thinking all turned on me and drove me to drink more and more, and in return I got a sentence of pain and suffering. The more I fought the demons, the worse it got. Alcohol, through my alcoholism, became my master. The physical consequences worsened, not to be outdone by the emotional, mental and spiritual collateral damage in its wake. It had to stop. And it did. So, then what? Happy ending, right?

Wrong.

Once I removed the booze, I was still left with the pain, the anger, the loneliness, the feeling of no worth and the hundreds of fears. Booze was the medicine. Now that I had no bottle-fed meds, I was hurting even more. Working through my program of recovery and inner work, I was able to jettison much of the festering flimflam that had seeped into my once beer-soaked pores. I was able to lighten the load and start the healing process. I made amends to those I had harmed and started to become a part of a fellowship of other alcoholics. I started to feel like a part of the human race, no longer needing people to toss flowers at me and no longer needing to feel useful and noticed. Like a hot air balloon, the more I tossed overboard, the greater and higher I soared.

Old ideas, old habits, old ways of thinking, old behaviours—the more I let go of these things, the more centred and free I am. My life today is about lightening the load, keeping it simple and getting down to the brass tacks of my life. Sounds easy, but it's not always so Deepak Chopra-tastic. So this simplifying of my life, this streamlining and this spiritual aerodynamic makeover is what I try to do on a regular basis.

For a few years, I was using a little netbook as my main computer. It had served me well, but slowed down to a crawl over time. No matter what I did—from removing files to using online tutorials to juggling settings—nothing seemed to speed up my machine. I had been tempted many times to smash it against the floor and be done with it. I had always dreamed of getting a new computer, but we didn't have the finances to do so. So I suffered with it. Someone then told me about Linux. I installed it and banished Windows from my computer. I had a brand new computer, quick and virus-free.

With Windows, I was running a system that was bloated, overwrought and not in tune with what I wanted or needed. I just required access to the internet, some music programs and some basic applications. I didn't need 800 fonts or systems so complicated and dysfunctional that they crowded my unit's space. I was using a platform that slowed down the simplest of tasks and commands by running all sorts of background programs and noise. Viruses and Trojans invaded at every step. My computer was full of things that no longer served it well.

That is precisely what I need every few months. I get to the point where things are bloated in my life. My physical health, my emotions and my mental capacity are all cramped and they run inefficiently. Like my old Windows system, I too am taxing myself, using up precious energy and time on things that are unnecessary or moot. I stall, freeze and drag. I am full of "stuff" again, like I was in my drinking days. I am jammed up with items that no longer serve me. I start to think in abstract 1s and 0s and find myself stuck in many ways. I find myself getting wound up about silly things, projecting my fears and insecurities on others. I start to drag myself down. I feel a spiritual deflation throughout my core.

So I make changes. I focus on eating healthier, recommitting to journaling and tackling neglected inner work. I focus on regular meditation, on reading more and on learning to let go of some of the things I hold on to. I exercise and move my body more. In making this new operating system switch in my own life, I find a whole different way of approaching things. I don't feel bloated and blocked as much. I feel lighter and more grounded, and my connection to the Creator feels stronger. I also feel more open and receptive. I have this sense that doors are opening in some ways. The Universe is responsive to our inner landscape.

Recovery is about change. It's about looking at things in a new way. It's about changing perception and tactics and seeking communion with the divine flow of this life. For me, it's not about not drinking anymore, although the goal is to leave this planet sober. It's about the life altering consciousness of my will in alignment with His will. It's about getting out of the way of my own life and letting it go to where it needs to go. My resistance to change is almost exponential to the quality of that change and its result. The more I struggle to change something in my life, the more I am holding on to an idea of my life that perhaps is no longer useful. The staleness that lingers on me, and the spiritual misalignment that follows, is usually because I am fighting something. In that whole equation there are the common denominators: fear and ego. Getting past these were the key to opening doors for me. It's frightening at times.

I know that no matter what crosses my path, I am not tethered to anything that will disturb me on a deep level. Surface things may be rough at times—lack of funds, poor health, etc.—but in the end, it's not the end of the world. The end of world was when I decided to put down the drink and step into a new world. In this world, I live a new life. In this world, I am surrounded by the Creator's children. In this world, I can close old windows, open doors and gaze at the Grace of God.

For a guy that wanted more, I get less. And I am ever grateful for that.

Loneliness – Community

"The eternal quest of the individual human being is to shatter his loneliness."
~ **Norman Cousins**

"Your duty is to treat everybody with love as a manifestation of the Lord."
~ **Swami Sivananda**

Eskimo Angels

He reeked of booze and body odour. The man I stood beside on the bus had a swollen and beaten face to match his scent. His dead eyes said it all. In his hospital-banded hand was a bag full of rattling Olde English malt liquor bottles. He stared into the distance while I sized him up. It was a reminder of where I came from and where I could be if I picked up again. I wanted to hug him, to let him know that it didn't have to be like that anymore. But I knew that look he had. He was long lost in his mind, his alcoholism and his perceived fate. He was, at that moment, a shell of what he could be and what he was meant to be. Was he one of us lost souls? An alcoholic with a capital "A"? I didn't know for sure, but I know most sane folk don't come back from the hospital and pick up booze before even removing the white tag on their wrist.

Someone later asked me if that man was perhaps an Eskimo Angel. I hadn't heard that term before but was glad I did. One common way to explain an Eskimo Angel is the classic tale of a man on a roof during a flood who prays to God for rescue. When a life raft and helicopter come, he refuses both because he says that God will save him. Finally, an Eskimo on a kayak offers to take him to safety, and again he maintains that he is waiting for divine intervention. After he dies and accuses God of not saving him, God tells him that he sent the raft, helicopter and Eskimo. The idea that the Creator works through others is the moral of the story, and it's something that I truly believe in.

Eskimo Angels are those who gently (or maybe not so gently) nudge and guide us towards living in the Sunlight of the Spirit. They are in the background and foreground. They pray for us, work with us, take our hand and help push us to the light of wellness. They may not even know they are Eskimo Angels. They may have no idea that they are in communion with the Creator to help someone get well. In the twilight of my alcoholic lifestyle, I know now that I had many Eskimo Angels around me, hoping for me and prompting and encouraging me to get well. I can look back and see that I had many, many opportunities given to me through others, to see just how bad a shape I was in. My denial, my ego and my alcoholism wouldn't let me see through the fog, though. But the Eskimo Angels did not relent.

I have had countless Eskimo Angels in my life, and some of them remain. My wife and parents. Friends. Ex-employers who tried to help me when they didn't know exactly what to do. Friend of friends who called me to share their experiences of getting well. Compassionate doctors and nurses who went above and beyond to get to the truth of my hospital visits. The people who called 911 when I was driving erratically. The police who gently took me off of the street and who played with my three-and-a-half-year-old in the car while his dad was in handcuffs. I didn't see them for what they were at the time, agents of the Creator, but looking back now I wouldn't be where I am now without them. These people helped me at precisely the times I needed them. I didn't orchestrate anything. The Universe did. Sure, my actions dictated my direction, but the outcome wasn't mine. In another dimension, I am in prison for life for killing innocent people with my car.

In this light, I don't begrudge or resent anyone who helped me in the ways they needed to help me, either by firing me, by arresting me, by pleading with me or by having other sorts of unpleasant exchanges with me. I am thankful for them and bless them daily. I have people in my life, today, who are no doubt continuing to gently prod me into greater growth, and I don't know that they are doing it. They are doing His work through their words and actions. I am affected by the cosmic touch of interaction via other humans. I am a bird who is riding the currents of the wind, being taken to where I need to go, without even knowing where that place is, wings spread but not flapping. The mosaic of this intermingled universal mass is much broader and wider than I can imagine. I am guided by voices that aren't my own yet that are a part of my inner landscape. The Creator within works through others without.

The wonderful thing about spiritual growth is that we never know if or when we ourselves become Eskimo Angels. A hug at the right time, a timely email, a welcoming phone call, an unexpected visit—these are just some of the countless ways that we can plant the seed of recovery and/or growth in others. How many times have you had the experience of saying or doing something seemingly small that resulted in someone telling you that the direction of their day or even life changed because of your action or word? We call it uncanny coincidence. I think of it as divine timing.

There are many ways that we can be beacons of light to those sitting in the darkness. Even just living a life of joy and contentedness can inspire someone to want what we have. It can be as simple as living by spiritual principles, using the laws of attraction. Sometimes it's just the way we carry ourselves, our energy, our smiles or our demeanor. These are ways we showcase the authentic self to others.

I now regret not hugging or talking to that man on the bus, or reaching out in some way. But many more people like him will come, I am sure of that. They remind me of what it was like and what it could be like if I drank again—the wreck of a runaway train. They are truly *my* Eskimo Angels because the Creator is holding a reflector to me, reminding me and also letting me know that I still have work to do. Carry the message. Help others. Get out of self. It's all His work. I'm just drifting by in my kayak.

Slow Ripening Fruit

I am not a good friend.

Let me rephrase that in a more positive light, in a new context and in a way that doesn't make me sound whiny and self-pitying, which is not the point of this writing. Here I go again:

I haven't learned to be a good friend. *Yet*.

Is that better? Does it resonate in a manner that is spiritually more grounded and closer to the intention of my spirit? I am not sure. But it speaks closer to my truth, rather than truth as we would like to express it, an iron clad-type commandment that is set in marble and recited as gospel at the light of the 10th Tempest Moon at late harvest. You know, *that* kind of truth.

Friendship and my struggles around it is an ongoing issue. It's one of those white dandelion tufts that flies in the air, gets caught up in the winds and never really settles. This is one of those core issues that seems to arise again and again, like perennials of the soul or weeds of the spirit. Every time I start to pin it down, I see something different, although it never really dissipates. Core issues are the things that still linger within me, that carry a residue long after I think I have it nailed down. Core issues are the sort of beasts that refuse to lie down, without a lot of work and examination. They are the old stories which do not like to go away.

Here is the deal with friendships: I often see solid, strong friendships around me. For example, my brother-in-law has a best friend, whom he has known since high school. They are both groovy cats. They have seen each other through thick and thin. They share much with one another, are present in each other's lives and are rock solid in their commitment to one another. They aren't inseparable, unlike a bunch of giggly school girls, but then again, they're grown men. And yet they share a spirit. They seem to complete each other and allow each other to step up, stand on the shoulders of one another and move through life's turmoil and joy together.

While bearing witness to this relationship, I have a hard time comprehending it. I get it, but I don't truly get it. *That's great for them*, I think to myself. A real measure of one's growth can be reflected on the mirror of a true friend, or at least that is the kind of thing they say when I look up friendship quotes online. Aristotle said, "Wishing to be friends is quick work, but friendship is a slow ripening fruit." Other dead folks have said motivational poster-type statements about friendship, too. There is the idea that a friend walks with you in the darkness, stays beside you despite faults and is there when others have abandoned ship. This almost looks good enough to investigate, but I'm not sure if I want to commit to that investigation, let alone delve into strong friendships.

Whoa, did I say the "C" word? Commit? This is getting complicated.

Growing up, I never really had true friendships. Sure, I had the occasional local kid who didn't mind killing time with me as we looked for grasshoppers and spiders. I had some acquaintances in grade school and I ran with some other disenfranchised brothers-in-arms while in high school, but I never had those guys who I bonded with in blood, or at the very least fake Halloween blood. I never carried a connection to my past, other than ancient resentments that helped keep me in the depths of my alcoholism. Friendship just didn't seem like it was in the cards for me. Who I had surrounded myself with for so many years weren't friends, but drinking pals and fellow bar stool warmers.

I do have some friends today. Well, let me qualify that. I have friends who started out as only my wife's friends. I think we all have those group of men and women who came along with our partners. Fellow travelers, all in coach. I have some very caring and kind-hearted people in my corner who saw both my wife and I through the rough spots of my bottoms and are still here today. Some of them visited me in treatment, some took care of me by taking care of my family while I was away. These souls are still with us today, and I am grateful. Outside of that, there aren't many people I can call friends who were propelled into my circle without my wife's assistance.

Let me make one thing clear, one thing that is very clear on my end after much inventory, discussion and deconstructive navel gazing: this whole thing is of my making. I am not a victim here. I am not wallowing in poor spirits over this (nor am I pouring spirits over this). I am staking a claim in something that I own and that bears down on the haunches of my life and my choices. To have a friend I need to be a friend. It's as simple as that. I haven't learned how to be—nor have I had the strong inclination to be—a friend. That clarity in understanding my role in this is where the buzz is. That's where the rubber hits the road for this wretched chimney sweep.

An old work acquaintance emailed me some time ago. He wanted to get together for coffee, something that he and I had bandied around for months. I ignored it. He emailed me again recently, declaring, "You can't ignore me forever. I'm a cool guy," half in jest. This sums up where I stand on things. I often "overlook" emails time after time and then wonder why I don't get emails anymore. I sometimes dismiss phone calls or any sort of attention where my presence is requested front and centre. I tend to squirm out of coffee dates and I avoid meal dates. I like the soft and easy approach to friendship—don't have any, or at least don't keep many. While that sounds rather brusque, I have to be fully honest and say that I just don't know any other way than that of the lone wolf. It's a predisposition of the mind, a strong echo of my old ways, leftover from my self-contained manner of living. My self-reliance has run down to another level.

This all boils down to one of my real truths, my real issues, which is that I want to be seen but don't want to be seen. I like the idea of being surrounded by those who like being around me and who see me for who I am rather than who I think I should be to them. I enjoy the visual of holding court with strong men and women who know me inside and out, who are there regardless of my character defects and unflattering flabby bits. What I don't see is putting my effort into it. As my wife has said to me over and over again, being a friend takes work. I have to *work* at this? Don't they all just come running up to you, tugging at your elbow, begging to be included in those reindeer games of yours? No? Oh. Am I ready to be there when one of my friends flame out in some part of their life? Am I ready to take calls at 4am and just listen? Am I prepared to drop what I am doing to be at a friend's side, *tout de suite*? Am I willing to put my egocentric ways aside and just be there for them? Call me selfish ("You're selfish, Paulie"), but I am not there right now because I don't know what it's like. I never went to camp for that. I didn't read the instruction booklet. I never got the pamphlet on how this shakes down.

I feel isolated because I don't have friends, but I am selfish, fearful and closed-minded about opening myself to others. I do want, but also don't want, others in my life, and then I wonder why I feel isolated and don't have any friends. I build my sandbox, create the borders up high so no one can come in, put in the toys, muck around in it and then wonder about the sand in my shoe, trying to read it like tea leaves. All I had to do was step out of the sandbox and play on the swings with the other kids.

I do find it difficult to open up to others. I take a very long time to trust and feel some sort of connection to someone else.

I can make fast, throwaway friendships hinging on the flimsiest of foundations. What I find difficulty with is making the soul-lifting, spirit-changing, full on bred-in-the-bone type of friendships. The concrete you can build condos on or launch rockets off of. Those folks or opportunities don't come often to me, and perhaps I have those in my life already and just don't see them. Or not. But in the grander scheme of things, what it comes down to is being where I need to be, getting clarity where I'm at and then deciding what actions to take. I do have choice when making my decisions. I am no longer the victim or the patsy, the stool pigeon or the dump site. So, I can introduce myself to someone or not. I can offer my phone number or not. I can muster up my courage and say yes to a cup of coffee at the local café, or I can turn it down to catch the bus home.

Friendship is a commitment, an ideal and a space in which I am learning to navigate. It's not something that comes naturally to me, but it's worth investing in. I am starting to experience the benefits of creating a bond with others without pomp and circumstance, without the expectations of anything in return. It's a process and it will bear some of its own fruit as I continue down that orchard path.

I can. I can. I can. But for now, let me get back to you on that coffee.

Redwoods

I remember the first time I took a writing course. It was a non-fiction class. I was nervous and was looking forward to taking my usual place in any classroom—in the back row, the closest seat to the door. It was the safe place, the equivalent of the ejector seat in an aircraft. When the pressure was too high and I felt I was going to crash and burn, I could release the switch and dart out of the room. I knew that no matter what, I had the ace in the hole to make a cartoon exit, smoke cloud and all behind me.

To my horror, the chairs were arranged in a circle. A circle. There is no escape in a circle. We all eyed each other. There was no hiding, no staring at someone's back. I felt vulnerable and open, which was symbolic as the writing assignments dealt with opening ourselves up for examination. The instructor pushed us to crack open our hearts and delve deep into our spirits. These were not the types of essays to write about what I did last summer. Lots of tears were shed, backs were pat and hands were held, and post-class hugs were common. It was the first time I felt safe in a room full of strangers. I felt less of a need to load up on booze before attending class.

Years later, I found myself sitting among strangers in church basements, also sitting in a circle. There was strong coffee in tiny Styrofoam cups and assorted cookies along the walls, which were adorned with 12-step banners and slogans. Sometimes these meetings were set up in a more traditional row system, but a circle is used when possible. The circle represents equality, wholeness, eternity, timelessness and even The Divine. I wasn't pouring my heart out in a personal story like I was in that writing class, but I heard plenty of other people talking about their struggles, their victories and their insights. I was just trying not to pour myself another double.

The symbolism of circles had me thinking about their power in man and nature. Specifically, it had me ponder over redwood trees. Redwoods are remarkable in many ways. Sure, we can drive an RV camper through some of them, but their uniqueness doesn't end there. For one, redwoods need fire to help them survive. They have bark up to 12 inches thick that acts like a heat shield when exposed to fire. So, while everything around them burns (and creates nutrients for the soil), they resist the fire. They are protected.

Redwoods also have a surprisingly shallow root system. You won't find many redwoods standing alone—their rootstock can't support it. But, when a group of redwoods grow in proximity to one another, their roots interweave, creating an incredibly strong base which can support the greatest and heaviest of trees. Not even over-saturated and soggy soil can soften the roots. The trees do not topple.

When a live redwood is knocked down for some reason, it will continue to grow through its limbs. If they can, the limbs will grow upwards, straight towards the sun. Often, a family of trees will grow out of the living remains of one fallen tree. Because these tree families grow out of the perimeter of the fallen tree, they form a circle. These circles are called cathedrals.

Redwoods make me think about how we plant ourselves in our communities, how we rely on one another and how we can't afford to hide away from others. I see how we move through the fire trials of life to find nourishment in the aftermath. I see how faith is in many ways my shield when the heat is on. I see how my reliance on a power greater than myself can protect me even when things are turning to ash around me, and how that ash encourages new growth once the smouldering fires have been extinguished. I look back at the times I had wished had never happened, but I realize now that I needed those flames. I needed the bush fire to rage around me, to cleanse me, to set the table for renewed hope.

I see the connection of the roots in the fellowships and congregations I am a part of. I have the experience of leaning on others and having them lean on me. When I interlock with others through friendship, love and service, I am stronger. They can support me when I feel like I can't support myself. We have a bond grafted underneath our collective conscious. We are greater than the sum of our parts. Our feet are rooted in faith and fellowship as we lurch towards the Sunlight of the Spirit. We grow from the experience and shared wisdom from those who have lighted the path before us. We form circles of healing and compassion around, and from, those who have fallen. The term "cathedral" itself invokes a sense of sacred space.

I alone cannot reach lofty heights. I need the help of others. I need their strength, their vision, and their know-how. When I have hit a plateau in my life, whether it be spiritual, professional or in any other respect, I know that tapping into someone else's energy will bring me to that next level. As much as ego would love to be the alpha tree upon the summit, watching the little saplings struggle below, I know that I need to be in the circle. I need to be a part of the tribe, the band. My success mirrors theirs and vice-versa. I tried to carry myself on solo power, and failed miserably (see related: the first 40 years of my life).

This healthy dependence on others also fosters much-needed humility. When my ego gets choked up in itself, it's because I have lost sight of the importance of community, of equality and of others. When I ask someone for help, I am tapping into that root structure, that energy source, that old growth. When I am able to be of service to another, the ground gets firmer beneath me, and I grow that much more.

I am grateful for the circles in my life. I am grateful to have the solidarity of my chosen community woven around and through me. I am grateful to see the forest.

Worthlessness – Hope

"To the world you may be one person but to one person you may be the world."

~ **Bill Wilson**

"Hope is the thing with feathers-
That perches on the soul-
And sings the tune without the words-
And never stops – at all."

~ **Emily Dickinson**

What is Your Favourite Colour?

Someone once made the mistake of asking me what my favourite colour was. We were in college, and a friend was doing a silly social "experiment," so she could tell you something about yourself with a few simple questions. It wasn't too far from those quizzes where you find out your drag queen name by using your first pet's name and the name of the street you grew up on. (I'm "Ziggy Jane," by the way. My wigs are as outrageous as my sass and hairballs.)

When I needed to confess my colour of choice, I blanked. I pictured the rainbow. I mentally tried to pull out a primary tone. Nothing came to me. My friend may have thought I was in precursor grand mal seizure mode, but I was merely colour blinded and bound.

"Purple?" I blurted out.

"Purple?" she replied, squinting at me. "Are you sure? You don't seem sure."

"Uh, black then?"

"Are you guessing? It's an easy question."

"Blue. Yes, blue! Oh wait..."

Science broke down right then and there. The experiment was over at the speed of cyan. I was unable to tell someone my favourite colour. If she had asked me who my favourite musician was, or my favourite season, I would have gone into zombie mode as well.

I couldn't access what my preferences were because I carried the fear of being rejected. I was always adjusting myself to who was around me. I was *very* much interested in what you thought of me and pulled every muscle to contort myself to your liking. Any sense of who I was eroded over time with every moment I made contact with other human beings. I wanted to fit in and be liked, so like a chameleon blending into its surroundings I changed according to the surrounding environment. If I was surrounded by jocks, I put on my Testosterone Teal game face. If I was hanging out with creative types, I flipped the channel to Vulnerable Violet sonnets.

Chilling with the drinking buddies? Well, let's put on the Brown Ale asinine smart-ass hat.

I learned to master the spectrum of façades to keep up with the crowd. The only problem was that I lost myself in those crowds. I was trampled underfoot. The more I tried to fit in, the more I shut myself off from me. Whenever I said something that I didn't believe in, I was white-washing my own spirit. I was betraying my authentic self. Eventually, I started to bleed out into faded hues and I lost track of who I was and who I wanted to be. I drifted.

I didn't know who I was any more. I was a mosaic of the last ten people I had run across. I was a Frankenstein's monster, slapped together with pieces from other people—mannerisms, expressions, interests, albums, clothing, work ethic, etc. Nothing was authentically mine. Even as I took on other people's skin, I was still an outsider. No matter how much I tried to be a part of, I was always apart from. I was the other person's understudy—close, but not the star others paid money to watch.

When someone asks me a simple question like what my favourite colour is, what I hear is "Who are you *really?*" It's like that scene in *Runaway Bride* where Julia Robert's character doesn't know how she likes her eggs. She always had what her romantic partner had. She had always tried to be who she thought her partner wanted her to be. When she realizes that it was not only destroying her but also her relationships, she decides to break out of the patterns. One afternoon she cooks eggs every way possible and tries each dish. She begins to learn how she truly likes her eggs. And that is how easy it is to lose ourselves in the stories we fabricate. For years, I didn't know that damn colour, nor did I know what my favourite dinner was, or who my favourite hockey player was, or even what I liked to read. I had to divorce myself from the palette of false selves and start with a clean canvas. I had to discover myself.

Learning to break out of the false self was, and continues to be, a challenge. The first thing I needed to embrace was the fear of not being liked. I had to understand that no matter what I did, no matter how much effort I put into trying to be Mr. Popular, no matter how I ripped myself apart to curry favour with others, there were going to be people who just didn't like me. One of my spiritual teachers explained this to me. He told me that I don't know that other person, what struggles they may be battling, and that perhaps I remind them of someone who hurt them once. Most likely, I remind them of something that they don't like in themselves, and regardless of what I do, they will react out of pain. Everyone responds to a different energy. We vibrate differently. Not everyone will jive with everyone. (If you consult your *Handbook of Humanity*, this is fact of life #467).

I also had to see that self-acceptance was the key into which I could walk through the door into my authentic self. When I understood that I was unique, that I was exactly who I was meant to be, that I was the vibrant person who was meant to shine and not be muted, then I could start to unravel who I was. I could acknowledge the true spirit within. As I honour that spirit, I start to feel freer. I feel more anchored within myself. I am no longer disloyal to myself. I am no longer smothering my truth. I am no longer lying. I don't feel the need to wear masks or squash down my quirks. I am less inclined to slip into perfectionism.

The irony of all this is that the less I try to fit into a particular crowd, and the more I shine as *me*, the more I find my true tribe. Like energy seeks like energy. I have found that the more I stick to my authentic self, the more open I am to others, and vice-versa. I have no need to pose as someone else. I have no inclination to falsify myself. I don't have to paint myself into a corner. I can just be and find genuine friendship and fellowship. And that is what we all seek: the comfort of being seen for our true colours and nothing less.

For the record, my favourite colour these days is green.

And yes, I am sure of it.

I'm Not What I Am Not

I am not a Type A go-getter. I am not a fighter. I am not a gardener. I am not a good singer. I am not a dancer. I am not good at debating. I am not gregarious. I am not a sharp dresser. I am not a beach person.

I can go on and on and clog the space around me with the things I am not, but I know from experience that it's a losing proposition to try and define myself by what I am *not*. It's an old scare tactic my self-pity liked to use to unleash a Level 10 Chuck Norris side kick to the head. Like the sculptor who tries to remove all of the stone that isn't an elephant to reveal the plucky pachyderm, I still find myself trying to carve away the "what I am not"s to reveal the real me. It's addition by subtraction, but it feels like the math is wrong. Zero plus zero still doesn't equal the One that I seek to be.

Tallying up all of the things that I am not just precludes anything from my life that may add value. I can say that I am not a handyman, and just leave it at that. Sure, I can screw in a lightbulb with the best of them, but outside of that I am a prime candidate for a seminar titled, "How not to Harm Yourself with a Hammer." I realize that in making a bold declaration of what I am not, or what I can't do, I put in my mind that I will never do it. If I reinforce the fact that I am useless with a wrench or screwdriver, then by the sword of Odin I will certainly find a way to fail at fixing a faulty faucet. I recall my brother-in-law being in the same boat as I am (a leaking boat that neither of us could repair, no doubt), so he took a series of classes at the local big box hardware store. He didn't go forth and build an ark in a fortnight or remodel the balusters at the Grand Duke of Luxembourg's summer house, but he instilled in himself a little confidence and skill for whenever he needed to make small repairs.

Limiting myself was as much conscious as it was unconscious. By detaching myself from the possibilities of growth and inclusion, I set off to prove that I was of no worth to others and myself. I made it a self-fulfilling prophecy to announce and stamp my ineptitudes onto my consciousness. By showing my cards and saying, "Well, that's pretty much it," I made sure that I left the poker table with an empty pocket and a spirit that was lightly crushed around the edges. The smell of burnt offerings often pulled me more into myself and away from the flame of life and all of its wonders. I was the referee of the game and I put myself in the penalty box for no other reason than because I wanted to step on the ice—not exactly a winning game plan. Whenever I listed the things that I wasn't, I limited my potential without knowing it. I simply thought that what I was whittling down wasn't me, but in fact I was whittling down what *could* have been me.

It's a human condition, I realize—this self-defeatist attitude. It's not the sole propriety of alcoholics or addicts. But for our peeps, this, like any other emotional or mental roadblock, bores down further, faster and harder into us, and affects us much more. We strike the oil of self-pity and demoralization a lot more often in the sandy shale of our spirits. I realize that I have to be careful when I compose an ad hoc compendium titled, "The Things that Paul Sucks At." It can easily pull me into the eddy of immobilization, the undercurrent of not being good enough. I have seen that when I start to flail there, I get sucked in more and more. Navigating these murky waters is dangerous stuff. It may sound a bit silly, this thing about naming off things we might not be great at, or about being honest with ourselves, but I know that when I start to get like that, I am sitting on the blurred lines of healthy introspection and unhealthy self-limitation.

This sort of ne'er-do-well thinking also seeped into my language and in my interactions with others. I often hid my true feelings by using euphemisms and Morrissey-like phrases (for example, "I am not unwell"). It was easier to tell you what I *wasn't* feeling or doing than to tell you what I *was* feeling or doing. It took the sting away from possible rejection. It put distance between you and me. How dare I get close to someone? It gave me a vagueness that allowed me to slip away from your radar. Telling you something that you couldn't grasp let me let you go, and then I blamed you for walking away.

It's like painting with white oils on a white canvas. Sure, there are some brush strokes, but they aren't adding up to anything other than gloppy clumps of distasteful work. Perhaps looking at it in a contorted way would allow a small shadow to form, but it was dubious at best. That is how I lived, fading away with no true colours showing, because I was too busy trying to recede rather than proceed. I saw others come to life in bold, bright swipes and dashes, a study of complementary hues and shades. I was envious of these self-portraits, of these almost fully conceived and executed works of art that breathed life into themselves. Brave and striking vermilions. Blushing and violent violet. I sat and watched, and

I said, "I am not those." Back to the canvas I went, pale palette in hand.

It's a gradual but important shift from "I am not this" to "I *am* this," to tether myself to something that is undeniably me, to see my reflection in the mirror and to take in who is there rather than who isn't. I am learning to see myself for who I am, and not for who I am not. Comparing myself to those things that I am not is folly. The only comparisons I can make is to myself, and to how much further I am in my personal path. I cannot afford the luxury of allowing my ego to build the scaffolding of a new edifice, a new panic room or a new shelter. I have spent time to dismantle the old ones, and I will continue to do so. I cannot hide behind what I am not.

I am still apt to present myself as something that I am not, to scurry into the shadows of no judgment, or perception of judgment. But the more I do that, the more inauthentic I feel. It's a sort of disloyalty, if you will, to the Creator who made me unique. To deny myself who I am and to speak to the authentic me is to deny the glory of my own self. Standing up and taking count of my blessings, talents and skills is not a vainglorious ego trip, but a shining of inner light and a cracking of the darkness of denial. Playing small does me no service, and it cuts myself off from others. I fear not who I am, but perhaps who I *can* be. When you're used to donning a cloak of invisibility, it's difficult to shed it and put on something that brings attention to who I am meant to be. Not shirking, but standing tall, humble yet comfortable.

I am not a good singer, but it doesn't stop me from singing in the shower or in the kitchen. It doesn't stop me from listening to the music, from humming along, from sharing it with others or from blasting it in the car. The things that I am not don't imprison me, but open the door to the things that I am and give me a shot at learning some new things, to open up myself to new experiences. I can take the path of claiming myself and staying true to myself, or I can run away and make claims on others, counting other people's blessings.

I'm not what I am not, and I am what I am.

For this, I am thankful.

Hideous Me, Glorious Me

"**Y**ou fucking idiot. Wake up you piece of shit." Calming, soothing morning words to myself, often spoken aloud for full affect. It had the sing-song cadence of a Russian war cry and all of the caress of a shot of brass knuckles to the solar plexus. The act of waking up was a disappointment in and of itself, and it my first failure of the day. I often wished for a quiet, quick death while I slept, but it seemed that God had a Bostonian "wicked haaaad" plan for me. I wasn't getting off the hook. One day I would have to take matters into my own hands. Until then, I had to scrape the old booze and sense of unworthiness off of my tongue.

Self-loathing takes effort; it doesn't come with an auto-install program. It takes concentration and time to whittle away any self-esteem or joy. It's not always easy to find ways to flay yourself or to give yourself a Full Nelson and suck the air out of your own chest. It's not always easy to cripple yourself. Self-hatred became my default mode. The neurons in my head started to fire and link up to create new pathways, which always pointed to the ever-growing "Paul The Dickhead" portion of my brain. Most times, I could not look in the mirror. I was often tempted to spit at my reflection and watch the hatred drip down the cold, hard surface.

It's a slow path, this idea of despising yourself to the core. We aren't born with this in our hearts. It's developed and engineered over time. I sometimes caught myself in the process of cussing myself out when I knew that an inch of self-forgiveness would have served me better, but the ego is relentless and it wants what it wants. Mine always wanted me down on the ground, mouth full of dirt and rat shit, ready to cry uncle. I could picture my ego high-fiving Freddy Krueger after slicing me down to size yet again.

The problem with hating yourself is that it cascades out. There is no love for others when there is no love within to draw from. I hated you because I hated me. I looked at the world with a negative slant because I was not on the level with my own spirit, if I even felt I had one. I was ruthless with others because I gutted myself on a daily basis. I left myself hanging for the vultures of prey to feast on and felt that I deserved it. I wanted to be punished, but I was sometimes too cowardly to do it myself. So, I got you to do it for me. I ripped at your flesh and waited for your inevitable retaliation.

At the same time, I wanted you to hold me, love me, and tell me that it was all going to be okay, but I didn't want you anywhere the hell near me. Get away, but hug me and fold me into you. Let me feel what a calm, beating heart feels like. I wanted to be seen for the soul beneath the creature.

There was always that duality involved, because there was the unfailing sense that there was still something worth salvaging in the smouldering dumpster fire I called my life. The ruby in the rubbish bin. I couldn't call it forth, but there was a small part of me that knew that there was more to me than the me I painted myself as. My authentic self tapped me on the shoulder and whispered that there was more to life than where I was at. There was a hideous me and a glorious me within. What I reflected was the dark, unhealthy, and hideous me. Glorious me was docked at the harbour, hoping to set sail.

It is never a clean Dr. Jekyll and Mr. Hyde deal—one doesn't go away for a nap while the other one comes out to play. There is an interplay between the authentic me and the false me. I never considered myself "evil" when I was in the throes of my alcoholism. My wiring wasn't "bad." I don't feel comfortable with those terms. But I *was* living an inauthentic life. I was not true to myself because I feared rejection and abandonment. My prior programming and need to conform thrust me into a position of living out the life of someone who wasn't truly me. And that set off a series of poor decisions, fantastic breakdowns in good judgment and a series of Benny Hill-like follies. The self-loathing was the low-level understanding that I wasn't living my glorious me. Hideous me, as I felt at the time, seemed to carry sway and sashay. But there were glimpses of my God-given glory always trying to push its way through the static. I had many moments where I would show that side of me, where I felt kindness and forgiveness, and those moments liberated and frightened me. I didn't know how to handle them. I feared being swallowed whole by them, and yet I craved to be authentic. It was grind churning between the two states.

My process of seeking and growing continues to show me that there will always be that false me lurking about. My pride and ego will feed it crumbs, and sometimes whole cupcakes with sprinkles (no less), so it will crop up and make poor decisions on my part. But I recognize when that false me is at work, and I can lasso that bronco down with some quick mindfulness, a change of perception, or by talking to someone about it. I can feel when I am blocking out the authentic me. It feels like I am being singed with the lash of self-hatred again—a feeling that I know well and do my best to avoid.

Learning to foster the authentic me is a lesson in self-love. It's about respecting the Divine in me and in others. It's about reflecting the intrinsic need to be of service and to live in a genuine state. It's about not shying away from who I was meant to be. It's about shining and stretching out. It's about playing large in the Sunlight of the Spirit.

Gloriously imperfect.

Compare and Despair

Do you know what's worse than doing something that is a no-winner? *Knowing* that what you're doing in a no-winner. It's like scarfing down a Costco-sized satchel of Fig Newtons and a pail of eggnog just before hitting Six Flag's new Vomitorium Ad Nauseum roller coaster. Often when I am ignorant about the foolish acts I perform, I am also oblivious to the true intentions behind them. It's a case of not knowing what I don't know. And that can work to my advantage, as that opens up the opportunity to grow. But until then, I still wear the dunce cap.

Comparing myself to others and not knowing it is like having the safety off of a gun. I am not quite pulling the trigger on something, but I do feel the cold caress of steel on skin and wonder why I feel off, angry, desolate and depressed. I can feel some sort of inner rumbling, like the puttering of an engine with the wrong fuel coursing through it. There is anxiety and a feeling of being ill-at-ease. When I am unconsciously comparing myself to someone, it puts me in a shoddy spiritual place. What's worse is when I *know* that I am comparing myself to others. Being in recovery and being more awake has given me the ability to see things with eyes open a little more than before, so I can clearly see when I am comparing and despairing.

We all know that comparing oneself to another is just one of those Oprah/Dr. Phil no-nos. There are some fantastic, deep thoughts on this topic that escape me right now, but I know they're out there. Religious and spiritual texts discuss this and countless articles have been written on the topic. We understand the mental, emotional and even physical consequences of doing this. Yet, a guy like me will still gorge on that food and hit that roller coaster ride. I hate eggnog, and Fig Newtons are yummy only in small bursts, but I will again and again engage in that behaviour and suffer the roly-poly aftermath. Mop and bucket, please. Pavement pizza, aisle seven.

When I was in treatment, I used to compare my bottom to those of the other guys in the recovery house. Hell, I was even envious of some of their stories. I remember confessing to everyone at a meeting about my envy of their fantastic tales of epic loss and dramatic takedowns. I wanted those stories. Mine were dull and tepid compared to theirs. One of the counsellors later pulled me aside and told me something that I never forgot: "You're where you're meant to be." In other words, I needn't compare myself to what these other men went through. Not many had the sordid, Raymond Chandler-like novella bottoms I imagined them to have. Most guys were like me, a stain on the bottom of a shoe. And I was too busy comparing shoe sizes to wipe off the mess.

Alcoholics and addicts didn't invent this comparison thing, of course, but we just happen to have deeper reactions to it. Like self-pity, jealousy or any of those self-induced and self-involved Rubik's Cubes that our minds like to fumble with, comparing oneself to others is something that should be left to those who can make a fast go of it and move on. It should be left to those who can treat it like a mental quickie, an emotional mile-high club entry. I tend to stick around it like an old college mate who crashes in your basement for too long. Comparison is toxic. It's another poisonous substance that flames through my veins and bangs up my serenity like Leather and Pinky Tuscadero at a tea social (hint: Google "*Happy Days* TV Show").

Comparison loves nothing more than to creep up on me

when I least expect it. The other day, I was riding my bike up a hill, at near top gear, and someone blew past me. Not another cyclist (I am used to that), but a skateboarder. A *skateboarder.* I might as well have had an old man shoot past me with his walker like an F-16 in an evasive maneuver over hostile territory. My mind went into meltdown mode and I compared myself out of any sort of peace I might have had. A skateboarder? What kind of cyclist am I? The pathetic kind, is the answer. Why can't I be one of those graceful, gliding cyclists who traverse miles and difficult terrain with the ease of a gazelle? Well, the reasons are simple, Mr. Compare Boy: You have Hobbit-like legs, you ride a heavy mountain bike, your bike is falling apart and your bike's tires are low on air. Simple physics, my wayward and lugging lad.

This has nothing to do with me as a person or as a cyclist, and has nothing to do with how "good" or "not good" I am. I know that intellectually, but somebody please tell the rest of me. The same goes for all of the other aspects of my life when I see someone achieve something that either I wished I had done or I didn't even know could be done. Let the record show that the comparison game isn't always about envy. Envy is when I get angry at someone for having something that I feel I should have or that I deserve. Envy is counting someone else's blessings. This is the "look at them, and now look at me" kind of reaction. This is not so much about what they have, but about what I don't have, whether I am deserving of it or not. It's my own will turning on me, ego feeding itself by chewing off its own leg.

Comparing things has its uses and times of use. Our minds are meant to compartmentalize, organize, prioritize, analyze and investigate to make judgment calls. This is useful when sizing up a new car, looking for an apartment, deciding on a job or even figuring out whether to go out with Terrence in Accounts Receivable or Todd in Shipping. Our minds are programmed to put things in certain orders and to shelve, file and place items in a mental database. But that same wonderful working of the mind will also want to do the same thing with people and other intangible and immeasurable things. My mind wants to make sense and sequence of the people that I interact with or bear witness to. My mind wants to put them in marching order like the Bradys or the von Trapps, and then give them ranking, like state fair cherry pies. Therein lies the danger.

While I can quantify objects, quantifying subjective and even intangible things ("He's more loved than I am!") is fraught with pitfalls. There is no way that I can make that leap and come out on top. It's like deciding what is more beautiful, a sunset or a rainbow? A baby's giggle or a lover's gaze? These are all completely different, and yet my mind wants to line them up with numbers attached to them. There is never a right answer, hence my ego wants to will itself to have the right answer. My default is that when it comes to me, I am at the bottom. So no matter what I have going on, whatever I have, it's never top notch. It must have an inner failing, like a blown gasket on a Lada. Comparing myself to incomparable things is a cosmic fail, yet I will rub myself up on it like a mosquito against a screen door.

Comparing myself to you takes away from me, and it takes away from you. When I compare myself, and I am on the short end of that comparison, I say that what I am, and who I am, is not important. I say that what the Creator has created is not of value, and that I have no worth. It sets in motion the wheels that I will eventually run myself over with, namely self-pity, jealousy and envy. I find myself emptying my mind of gratitude. I lose sight of the talents, skills and abilities I do have and blather on about what I don't have. I also place you on a pedestal, which is unfair. I don't know the struggles you may have had to get to where you are. I am flippant about your journey, and that devalues you as a person.

When I dig deeper, I see that comparisons and the inevitable conclusion that I am not good enough bring me to a place of fear—the fear of being rejected. And that's a heavy trip, a Wavy Gravy kind of trip.

When I saw that skateboarder pass me, it wasn't just about me being slow. It had hit that bedrock of "I am not enough." I thought that no one will like me because I am not flying through the streets at Mach 3 speed. No one will like me because I am not a virile and strong man. No one will like me because I don't like me right now, and who wants to mess with this trash bag called Paul? So, while I may not travel quickly on two wheels, I can certainly break down my serenity in lightning fast time. That feeling of being rejected is a core issue for many people, and it will play out in this comparison game I have going. There is only one way to manage this.

I need to see and feel that I am good enough. The idea that I am enough is a tough one for me to tackle, even to this day. To think that what is here, right now and in the place I am, is more than enough? Slap me silly and call me Sally, because this is news to me. I had a whole lifetime of feeling less than others, so to prop myself into a spot where I am on the same level as others, like that little bubble on a carpenter's level, will involve a lot of heavy spiritual, mental and emotional lifting. Remember what I said about having squatty legs? Well, they come in handy, and now I am ready to lift. Just, not all at once. I don't want to break my back. It's by this lifting and by sensing that I am neither lesser than nor greater than others that helps to line me up with the Creator's will. It brings me to the path of freedom and serenity. It's a way of being that is still hard for me to bear at times, because that small voice that says "You're not worthy" still likes to prod and poke at the bear inside me. But, I am aware of the voice, and this awareness always helps to neutralize the hordes at the gate.

I think we all can write a list of all of the things we don't have, can't have or even shouldn't have. We all can consciously and unconsciously align ourselves against some impossible measuring system and still fall short. We all can see the futility of it all yet still go back to the very thing that brings us to futility. At least I can. But, what is the point of all this? It's wretched navel-gazing that bears no fruit of its own except a temporary sick spirit. Comparing myself to you is like letting a bird go free and then yanking it back down with a wire attached to its leg. Whenever I compare, I am denying myself the ability to soar and to glide with the sun bearing down on me, the wind lifting me up and guiding me. I ground myself and wonder why I am not free.

In my final analysis, I am me and I have to get used to that idea. I have to see that I am enough and that the only one I can compare myself to is me. I can see where I have come from and where I am now. And right now, I see a lot of leaps and bounds between the old Paul and the one typing these words.

I have good qualities. We all do. I also have my limitations. We all do. So why linger and let my mind burn holes in my soul when I can spend that energy helping others or staying close to the Creator? But, my mind likes to play, so the comparing will occur. I know it will. But I can lessen the damage as I am increasingly more comfortable with me. I can play in the Sunlight of the Spirit rather than plunge into the darkness of the well. I am good enough. I am good enough. I'll get there.

I am just a bit slow, remember? But I'll get there.

Peeking Through Joy's Window

My oldest son loves to run. Not just a playful kind of run that little kids engage in, but a divinely inspired kind of run that demonstrates his love to run. He tires out well-conditioned nannies and caregivers (including me). He can outrun and outlast kids almost twice his age, smiling as he crests over bumps and ducking under outstretched bush limbs. He's half gangly legs, half goofy grin.

A few years ago, he was running down a hotel hallway towards the elevator. My wife, our youngest and I tried to keep up. When we finally caught up to him, my wife turned to our now panting kid and said, "Yusef, I think when you run, you are closest to God," and gave him a peck on the top of his sweaty head. At the time I didn't think much of that comment, but it slowly started to seep into me. Those deep words played in the shadows of my mind.

When I think of my son running, I feel the true happiness it gives him. It's like his spirit does truly soar, even if only for a moment of two. I see that same soaring of spirit in my youngest when he discovers something again but reacts as if it's his first time seeing or experiencing it. When he wrinkles his nose and bursts out with that great belly laugh of his, I feel that he is closest to God at that moment. It's like there is a brief, undisturbed, uncontrolled, unwavering, profound glimpse into something that we are only privy to in sacred moments. This something produces a light within us that can only exude out towards others, be caught like a ripple in a pond and brush up against us without us knowing exactly what it is. But we know that we have been touched. It's something I can only describe as peeking through joy's window.

I often spend time looking at people—folks at work, on the streets, in cars—and I wonder what it is that they do that allows them to peek into joy's window. What is it underneath the uniforms and masks of modern living that sends them to furtively glance through the window? Do they even know that they are peeking? When I spy an old man navigating through a crowd with his walker, I often picture him as a young man—slapping his chums on the back, tugging at his girlfriend's sleeve, sneaking a kiss—playing at something that brings him close to what he only approaches when his mind and spirit are in alignment with the Creator's. What am I seeking when I look at that old man? Do I seek that very thing in myself?

When I was a young boy, there were things that had me peek into joy's window. I used to read a lot, listen to music, play games and play sports. I loved homework and doing well in school. I enjoyed hanging out with adults and I tried to act grown up. I tried to mature faster. Why I was in a race to leapfrog over my childhood, I don't know, but I enjoyed lapping it all up. It was a rush.

Over the years, I tried to blot out those fragile memories. Alcohol was like a huge magnet, wiping out the remaining fading memories of my younger days. I used to think that alcohol could bring me to a place of contentment, of bliss and of rapture. I could drink and actually feel what it was like to feel again, like I did as a child. I felt what it was like to be happy for once, to pick up the loving vibes from the room and to feel more comfortable in my own skin. I truly felt that I was peeking through joy's window. But it was a façade. That window I thought I was facing was only a picture of a window—one-dimensional and quick to disappoint. Drinking brought me to the general vicinity of happiness and elation, but like a wisp of smoke it was impossible to capture. I could never hit that mark, no matter how hard I tried.

What brings me utter joy is not easily captured by one singular event. It isn't necessarily a thing I do or an act I perform, like gardening or skydiving, but a state. I don't live in joy every moment of my life, but I live in gratitude for most of it. I find myself peeking into the window unexpectedly, like when my kids make me laugh or when someone tells me that I helped them out in some way. I peek when I run on a trail and marvel at nature. I don't know what it is that will tap me on the shoulder and bring me to that place of being closer to God's abundance of joy.

I am content to continue watching others peek through joy's window and see their total surrender of self to pure love and utter completion for those moments. I am content to watch my sons run and chance upon life and laugh and know that it's a lifelong pursuit. The window is always there if we keep our eyes open for it.

Acknowledgments

I would find myself in another fine mess if I didn't first and foremost thank my brother-in-law, **Ish Khan**. He harassed me for years to write a book and I often dismissed him as being a nutcase, which is partially correct. But his madness wore me down. His loving persistence planted the seed for this collection. He and his amazing wife **Josie** have always been supportive and for that I thank them. I also want to thank my nieces **Sophia** and **Ava** for their love.

I would also like to thank **Marnie Kay** at **Meraki House Publishing** for her wonderful guidance and abundant patience in helping to shape this book. Her optimism and feedback was both greatly appreciated and valuable.

I would like to extend gratitude to **Karen Brook**, who in her own gentle (and sometimes not-so-gentle) ways, helped to keep me on track with this goal. Her encouragement inspired me to continue pressing forward.

I want to thank **Melina Breault** for taking my hot mess of a manuscript and transforming it into an entity that I am proud to hold. Her prodding questions and keen eye kept me honest.

I want to give a loud shout out to my fellow recovery writer comrades. They lifted me up when I felt like quitting, answered my dozens of annoying questions, and inspired me by their own fantastic writing. In particular I want to thank **Daniel D. Maurer, Mark David Goodson, Claire Rudy Foster** and **Sean Paul Mahoney** for being the beautiful and talented souls they are. I also want to thank **Olivia Pennelle, Jake D. Parent** and **Kristen Rybant** for their wondrous work and friendship.

I also want to thank everyone in the online #recoveryposse group and the sober bloggers entourage. Without you this wouldn't have been birthed. You continue to teach me love, humility and what it takes to move through life with grace and dignity.

Finally, I want to give thanks to all the men and women who have lighted the path ahead of me on this passage, and to those who are starting their own journey of recovery and healing. Bless you all.

PAUL SILVA
- AUTHOR -

An avid reader and composer of short stories, **Paul** lost himself in words and music while growing up, until he started to lose himself in bottles and shot glasses. As a professional chef, Paul worked long hours and found a home in the hospitality industry after-hours activities. He continued to write and start a family, until alcohol took over.

After countless bottoms and a dismantling of his life at the hands of booze, Paul finally cried uncle at the age of 40 and promptly went into detox and treatment for his alcoholism.

Since then, Paul has been very active in the recovery community. He also started a popular recovery blog, Message in a Bottle, and has written regular blog posts for Sanford House and several guest blogs.

In addition to his writing, Paul designed a recovery podcast, Buzzkill Pod, in which he explores spirituality and recovery in all its various flavors. His Buzzkill Pod website was listed as one of the Top Ten Recovery Websites by The Fix magazine.

When not writing or speaking about recovery, he can be found stepping on LEGO bricks, snacking between meals, or running. He currently lives in Toronto with his wife, two boys, and a dachshund.

*Publishing with
Soul, Creativity & Love*

Meraki House Publishing, founded in 2015 has established its brand as an independent virtual publishing house designed to suit your needs as the Author, delivering the highest quality design, writing and editorial, publishing and marketing services to ensure your success.

"Where your needs as an Author have become ours as an independent Publishing House."

WWW.MERAKIHOUSE.COM

In partnership with
www.designisreborn.com

Copyright 2017, Meraki House Publishing

Marnie Kay, Founder & CEO
marniekay.com

CPSIA information can be obtained
at www.ICGtesting.com
Printed in the USA
LVHW110313040220
645693LV00001B/70